Still Laughing

How did I end up here?

Linda John-Pierre

Still Laughing: How did I end up here?

ISBN: 978-1-7392281-0-1 (Paperback)
ISBN: 978-1-7392281-1-8 (E-Book)

Cover and interior design: Andy Meaden meadencreative.com

Editor: Simon Monk

Front cover photography: theheadshotbox.com

First printing edition 2022.

Contents

Preface

This is an insight into the lady who grew up in a very humble, loving, supportive, funny and happy home.

Her story is written unapologetically and with as much humour as possible, even through the darkest times of her life.

Not knowing where life's adventures would take her, what has happened along the way, and how Linda grew bigger balls than some of the men she's encountered along the way.

The message here is one of transparency while it also contains snippets of her personal and professional life. The highs and the lows, the laughter in between and ultimately the message of hope.

She's accomplished a lot over the years and felt it was time to share some of the stories that have kept her going: the challenges, the frustrations, dealing with TWATS (There We Are Then Sweeties), coping with anxiety and depression… But have no fear, it's not all doom and gloom, there's plenty of humour too…

You'll also find stories from friends and business associates who have known her over the years, which offer a new perspective into the life and times of Linda.

About the Author

Linda John-Pierre was born in 1968 and raised in East London by her Dominican parents (Anastasia and Abner John-Pierre), who have lived in London for more than 50 years. Linda is the youngest of three daughters. Also known for her (very loud) laugh, upbeat personality, positivity, purple hair and being grateful for LIFE! She has worked her way up from very humble beginnings and wanted to share some of the harrowing and joyful times with you all. Linda now resides in Liverpool and London.

Mum and Dad, taken September 2022 in Dominica, West Indies

Dedication

This book is dedicated to my mother and father who have shown me nothing but unconditional love, support, words of wisdom, encouragement and truth on my journey into the unknown within the entertainment industry I have chosen to work in. Thank you for making me the person I am today.

To Chanel, who has always been at the end of the phone, through the good times and the challenging times. The Number one champion who continues to show unwavering support in all that I do.

To Karime aka (KK) Thank you for being my sister from another mister, my very own psychologist and keeping shit real with me. Encouraging me to get my book started and for the continued voice notes (Good morning, Good morning, Good morning)!

To Liverpudlian Lorraine! You know who you are! Thank you for speaking affirmations so positively especially asking the Universe to continue helping me to book the next job! You are an Angel and I will always be grateful for your kind words of support.

To the friends I call my true sisters, who have always been at the end of a voice note, a phone call, an email and a text message. Thank you for listening to my crazy WhatsApp responses which have sometimes gone into podcast mode because the message has ended up being so long, yes, sometimes at least 20 minutes! Lord knows what I have to say!

Ann and Abner John-Pierre, Linda's Mum and Dad

My earliest memory of Linda singing was when she was around two years old. She was singing a Stevie Wonder song, I can't remember the song but I thought, 'She's not long started talking and how does she know all the lyrics to that song?'

Linda has always had a passion for singing and the arts. Her father and I believe she inherited her gift from her grandparents on her father's side of the family. They all loved to sing.

We would agree that Linda's talent stemmed from her father's love of singing too. He was in a band back in the 1960's and in today's world, they would've been called a 'boyband'.

Singing and performing arts were always in Linda's blood. It has never left her. Linda has gone on from entering singing competitions when she was 16 years old, through to appearing in television shows like Stars In Their Eyes and Michael Barrymore's My Kind of Music.

Even when she fell pregnant at 15 years of age, whilst at secondary school, this never deterred her from following her dream. It was a difficult time for all of us in the family, however, we got through the tough times and we have our gorgeous granddaughter (Chanel).

Back in those days, when Linda was so young, we didn't know anything about how to push her in the right direction in terms of performing arts training. If we had known what to do and how to do it, we would have ensured that she attended a performing arts school so that she could learn the craft.

Linda didn't receive any academic training in performing arts, but this never stopped her from following her dream.

We have always encouraged Linda (and her sisters) to follow what's in your heart and her dream has always been to entertain. She was always the one who would be singing around the house or doing a different accent, which always had me and her dad laughing and she still makes us laugh today.

It's not always fun at some of these productions either (theatre mainly) – we're not sure why there seems to be so much more negativity within a theatrical environment. We thought everyone loved to be there because they're working on something special.

Linda would tell us things that made her very sad whenever she worked in theatre (not all theatrical jobs were riddled with drama). She was subject to bullying, intimidation and was ostracised whilst working on productions. This was a very low time for Linda. She didn't want to leave the production because she feared being blacklisted by casting directors and directors and there may not have been understudies to cover the role. So she had no choice but to get on with it.

The last time Linda felt incredibly low was when she did Showboat in the West End – she hated it. The show was brilliant, but Linda couldn't wait to tell us when the show announced they were closing only three months after opening at the Gillian Lynne Theatre. Linda chose not to work within theatre for three years after her time at Showboat.

It's heart-breaking to see anyone's child go through such sad times in an industry they love.

Linda had her baby at 16 years old and we still allowed her to live an active social life even though she became a new mum. We didn't want to restrict her life any further than necessary.

I wanted her to find a 9-5 job because she had the responsibility of being a full-time mum. But Linda being Linda, she started working nine months after Chanel was born.

Linda has worked hard in both office jobs and in entertainment. Even when she moved to Liverpool on her own, we thought she'd gone mad, but she's shown us that she's not afraid of taking risks and continues to live her life as positively as possible.

The moment I realised that she should give up the 'day job' was when the whole family saw her in The Billie Holiday Story and she played Billie Holiday's mother in Act 1 and Ella Fitzgerald in Act 2.

We were truly blown away at how different the characters were that Linda played, and the songs she sang within the production.

As soon as the show was finished, we met her in the foyer of the theatre and I told her then: "Girl, this is what you are meant to be doing!"

We've seen Linda in so many productions we cannot remember them all, however we've always given constructive criticism about her performances and the show itself. We don't see the point in boosting her confidence when she's such a confident person anyway. Linda is aware that we would always be honest with her regardless of the project or who she's worked with.

I'd like to think we have helped keep her feet firmly on the ground.

We are getting on now, and so it's a little bit difficult for us to continue seeing Linda in the productions she's involved in. We enjoy watching her on television in the commercials and any of the soaps.

The last theatrical show we've seen Linda in was Mamma Mia! The Party which was at the O2 in North Greenwich. Another great show and Linda had a great part playing Debbie. I've always said to Linda's dad that Linda is more or less being herself, so that's nothing new!

There's not much more for us to say at this point because we could speak about our Linda forever and what she has done within her ever-expanding career.

To say we are so very proud of our girl is an understatement. The entire family are so proud of her too.

She has achieved so much and we believe she has so much more to do within this industry that continues to set her soul on fire.

Love Mum and Dad x

Introduction

Jo Henry,
Actor & Friend

What can I say that's not good about this lady… but let's start with how we met…

I'm on holiday with my hubby Tim, and I happen to check my emails (at this point I've been looking after myself on the creative front, except for the commercial agent I was with, and it's been very quiet on the audition front for two years). The email said they were looking to fill a gap in the books with more mature actresses, and having seen my profile, would I like to join her for a meeting. I think I messaged that I was away and would contact them on my return.

I do a little research and find it's a small agency with a select group of people, and I book to pop along and have a chat; after all the office was only a 10-minute drive from me.

We have a very long chat and had quite a bit in common. We both have Caribbean heritage, and we are similar in age. We chat about our families with humour and a familiarity that you have when your parent/parents come from a Caribbean background. I thought Linda was lovely, and I'd made a promise to myself only to have an agent that I could get on well with.

While waiting to speak to her I'd looked at pictures of her present clients, and apart from a lady I recognised from my past touring days. I knew no one else. Having talked for nearly two hours; the ever-careful person that I am, said I'd be in touch when I'd had a think. I'd had agents in the past who just didn't have my interests at heart, so I wanted to mull it over.

On the same day, I'd got a commercial casting in Goodge Street, and a small theatre audition that I'd found myself. As I exited the casting, on the corner of the street was a gin bar that had outside seating and sitting there was a face I recognised as one of Linda's clients that had been staring at me from her wall. I asked if he was, and got a yes!!! I then asked what she was like, and he had nothing but a glowing review to give. Comments like, 'Lovely lady, you'll love working with her, great energy'. Well that decided me, I said yes, and let me tell you what that did.

Linda has an energy that is infectious, whether you are on the phone or with her in person, and I'm sure that bubbles over to casting directors too, and that can only be a positive thing. Within a year I had new photos and some great work under my belt. Started with a part in Vera with a nice little scene with Brenda Blethyn. Wonder Woman 1984, Trigonometry, Last Christmas, and finally on parting company (a career change for Linda had presented itself) she said how about we find one more casting as a farewell. Well, that casting was BRIDGERTON and the rest is history!

Linda has changed my career and has done more for my career in the short time I was with her than anyone previously. She's also a friend, while my husband and I have been to see her perform live and WHAT A VOICE!! And when schedules allow we meet, or chat over the phone about life, work and family. She always shows an interest in what you are up to, and throws encouragement to whatever new project you've signed up to. Some people shine bright, and this lady does just that.

1
The Early Years (2 to 10 years old)

Keith Strachan
Director, Musical Director, Musical Supervisor, Composer

I first met Linda in 1999. I was auditioning some girls for a show I was putting together called The Blues Brothers Meet The Soul Sisters. I had this idea that each of the three girls would sing the songs of Tina Turner, Aretha Franklin and Diana Ross respectively. I was having real trouble casting a girl to sing Aretha.

There was a nice girl (Natalie Tinn), who auditioned - she had a lovely voice but not really what I was looking for. I said to her, "You've got a great voice but I really need a girl who sounds like Aretha Franklin." And this lovely generous girl said, "I know exactly who you need. I have a friend called Linda John-Pierre who has the voice you want."

I said, "With a name like that, is she French?" and she laughed and said no, she's a Londoner. So she gave me her number and I called her and she agreed to come to audition at my house. I should say that I had no expectations – I'd seen a lot of girls by then and Linda was just one more. At the allotted time Linda arrived at my house and my wife Jennifer showed her up to my studio.

She stood there and I remember she had this wide smile and an infectious nervous laugh (she laughed a lot). I liked her immediately and asked her what she'd like to sing. I can't remember if she brought music, but I do remember playing You Make Me Feel Like A Natural Woman, a song written by Gerry Goffin and Carole King for Aretha Franklin. I can remember the moment to this day 23 years later. I played the intro on my piano and Linda began to sing behind me.

The hairs on the back of my neck stood up at the sound that came from Linda's mouth. She had such a great gospel sound. It was like being in the room with Aretha herself. You can't fake that sound – the singer has to live and inhabit that world to even come close. We finished the song and I applauded and she laughed long and loud. "Sing it again," I said. And she did. It was joyous. "The job's yours," I said. "Can you start Monday morning?" And she laughed long and loud one more time.

We had one week's rehearsal as I recall and, back then, Linda had very little theatre experience so I remember the rehearsal period being quite stressful for her. She had to learn a lot of backing vocals which was new to her so this added to remembering dialogue, where she came on stage, where she stood for this song and that song – Linda was like a rabbit in headlights for that first week. There was not so much of her infectious laugh during that week. But then, when the show opened and she was required to do her thing – stand on the stage and sing all those Aretha Franklin songs with an eight-piece band – that's when Linda shone.

The audience loved her and Linda relaxed a little thereafter – the infectious laughter returned. The show toured for a few months and by the time it finished Linda had become a seasoned pro.

I worked with Linda again a few years later in a show called All You Need Is Love which had a run in the West End. It was a show comprised completely of Beatles songs but performed differently to the originals. Linda closed the first half with a wonderful gospel version of Let It Be.

At the tender age of two years old, I could be heard singing in the dining room. My mother noticed that I was singing a Stevie Wonder song. She was a little shocked because at the time, I was still grappling with the English language! Songs were always played in the John-Pierre household, particularly at the weekends.

This is a memory which stays with me because my father lived for his music and entertainment. I was born in March 1968, a sensitive yet happy upbeat soul who would always love to laugh (loudly).

I can remember whenever we visited friends and family, if anything was remotely funny, I'd be the one laughing the loudest. Either my mum or dad would be the first ones to say, "Linda, you're making too much noise!" Would I take any notice? Like fuck I would! In my head, if something was funny, make sure you laugh out loud with the most joy!

I remember my first ever visit to the theatre. We watched a show called Ipi Tombi. This was back in 1976 and the show was in a West End theatre. It opened in 1974, in Cape Town, South Africa and was written by Bertha Egnos Godfrey and her daughter, Gail Leakier, telling the story of a young black man leaving his village and young wife to work in the mines of Johannesburg. The show closed on Broadway in 1977.

My parents purchased seats in the gods, because I remember thinking, 'It's taking a long time to get to our seats!' I was utterly blown away by the cast. Obviously being such a young age, I couldn't remember the storyline, but it was the music, the drums and the costumes which left me speechless and all I could think of at the time was, 'I need to be on stage doing what they're doing'. I believe I spoke about the show for a further two weeks because I enjoyed it so much. Actually, I loved it!

That's where the fuel was added to my inner fire. I knew that I'd love to be on stage singing and dancing, but I didn't know how I could make this happen. In the meantime, I would listen to the radio and watch Top Of The Pops. I'd be singing along to the songs and annoying everyone in my household whilst they were trying to watch the programme in peace!

I would be that child who would be in my room singing along to almost every song on the radio, when I should've been doing my homework. Everyone knew I was at home because I was always either singing or laughing. This passion for music grew so much that by the time I was ten years of age, my father suggested I join a choir. At that age, I thought I knew it all and in an instant, I rejected the idea! What the fuck does a ten-year-old child know? However, my father didn't push any further and left the final decision in my hands. Obviously now, I look back and think I should've joined the choir because I could've learnt so much from them, even learning how to read music or play an instrument. I still can't do either of those things!

My father has always been my inspiration to sing. I heard this story many years ago and I thought I'd share it with you. When my parents had settled in the UK, they had both found jobs and were doing okay for themselves. My dad was in his prime and he loved singing. He joined a five-piece band and was the lead singer. The band had their first-ever gig at a wedding and people were beginning to hear about them and how good they were. The day of the wedding came and the band were ready to perform. One of the family members asked him what the band name was and they didn't have one. So they had to be announced as The Band! They went down a storm and everyone loved them. They sang all the classics and had everyone singing and dancing along.

It wasn't long before the band were getting a really positive name for themselves. Soon enough they were approached by a man who wanted to manage them and take them on a European tour. The band couldn't believe their luck. However, my sister and I were around two and three years of age and getting babysitters to look after us whilst mum and dad went to work was sometimes a challenge in itself. However, they always found a way of getting someone to look after us so that they could go to work.

My mother was pleased for my dad, however, she gave him an ultimatum and said: "If you leave to go on tour with this band, you will never see your family again." My dad had to make an executive decision and very quickly.

He decided to stay with his family and find a permanent job in a Jewish food wholesalers. So the hunt was now on to find his replacement. My dad found a young girl, who was around 15 years old. He said her voice was like an angel and the rest of the band thought so too. The only issue here was that she was so young and her father didn't agree to her leaving to go on tour with four male members. In the end an agreement was reached and the young lady headed off with the band to tour Europe.

A few days before they were due to leave, my dad bumped into the band at the local petrol station – they were on their way to the airport to start their European tour.

They said they still wanted him to join them, but he explained why he couldn't go. They wished each other well and they went their separate ways.

The band went on to become very successful throughout Europe. We never did find out what they ended up calling themselves!

My father then settled into full-time employment and stayed at home to care for his family. In the meantime, he was always singing around the house too! At most opportunities my parents would take us to the theatre to see shows, including a pantomime each year at Stratford Theatre Royal East. This was a real treat! As mentioned earlier, music was always being played in the family home particularly over a weekend when both my parents would be home.

This was so joyful for me because we never knew what my father or mother would choose to play. Their music taste would range from Stax Atlantic, Motown, Elvis, Jim Reeves, reggae, soca, R'n'B, blues, soul, and various other genres which would have all of us in a good mood, singing and dancing in the kitchen.

Sundays were more peaceful with Christian and gospel music being played. It was a day of worship so things were much more chilled out. Sundays were also the day my mum would feed the five thousand with her humungous West Indian roast dinner. This would include roast lamb, fried chicken, rice and peas and plain rice, roast potatoes, vegetables, macaroni cheese, salad, coleslaw and fried fish and on a good day, we'd have fried dumplings thrown in too! My mother's love language was definitely good wholesome home-cooked food and we loved it. This was how me and my sister were taught how to cook. Before we left for school, my mum would say, "Okay, so when you two get home from school, start the dinner and when me or your dad get home, we shall finish off cooking it." My sister and I would always try and dispute what she said, but my mother had a point stating, "Well, do you want to have dinner tonight?" I think you can guess our answer! This made us become great cooks and we both still love it to this day. So thanks Mum for helping us create our culinary skills!

Fast forward to being a ten-year-old with a voice! My parents knew I had a voice but didn't quite know or understand how to channel this talent into a performing arts arena. Back then they didn't know about performing arts institutions which I could've attended, so we didn't pursue anything further because we didn't know where to look. One thing is for sure, I loved play-acting and once I started secondary school, I loved drama (both the subject matter and the friends I'd be amongst who would create their own dramas!).

2
The Teenage Years

Kim Jones
Lifelong friend

I first met Linda back in the 90s when we were studying counselling and psychology.

This is where I first got a taste of her entertainment side, when we all gathered at her flat in Stratford and watched her on TV performing as Chaka Khan on Stars In Their Eyes.

From there on, I've seen her do theatre, TV, films, cruises, musicals and various other entertainment pieces.

One thing I can say about Linda is she is not work-shy. Her motivation and encouragement from her friends and family keep her going.

If I had to sum Linda up, it would have to be her laugh. It is so infectious and you can't help but laugh with her. I thought it was just her until I met Glenda (Linda's cousin) at one of her shows. It must run in the family!

She is very family-oriented and the bond between her and her daughter Chanel is incredible.

She has a heart of gold and remains humble throughout. My girls love her and always fondly call her Aunty Linda and ask when she's going to be on TV next.

I am honoured and blessed to have her in my life. I'm always excited to see the next chapter of her journey.

What happened next?

Who knew how things were going to take a dramatic twist when I fell pregnant at 15 years old. Yep, the first time I ever had sex and the next minute, I'm expecting a baby. You really could not make this up. However, my daughter is the best gift any mother could ever wish for!

So, here I am cheggers preggers at 15 years old. I knew I was pregnant, but it took my mum three months to realise, plus whenever my mum dreams of fish, she will hear about someone she knows or knows of who is going to have a baby. Yes, she was dreaming about fish a lot but little did she know it was her youngest child who was carrying a child. My daughter's father never wanted to take responsibility for his own flesh and blood, which is a shame because he missed out on so much of her life and all the things she has achieved.

My dreams of wanting to go into the entertainment industry were crushed. I thought at the time, 'This is it'. I might as well continue to study and get a 'normal job' in an office to look after myself and my baby. Don't get me wrong, the fire ALWAYS burned deep within, in terms of dreaming about working within the entertainment industry. But I had a child to look after and my singing would have to remain on the back burner for a good few years.

So in the meantime, I would sing at friends and family weddings, christenings and funerals just to keep that spark alive.

Believe it or not, expecting a child at such a young age had its advantages and disadvantages. The advantages were, I was the first pupil from my secondary school to receive home schooling. I felt for the teacher who would visit our family home to attempt to teach me a multitude of subjects including Home Economics (cookery) in my family kitchen which went down like a lead balloon. Not a successful lesson at all. Either the things we attempted to make ended up being burnt, or were under-cooked.

I was also still allowed to live as normal life as possible as a teenager, going to nightclubs and youth centres to stay connected to friends from school.

In the end, I still failed miserably in all of my CSE exams. Nearly all of them were unclassified. I remember the thought of trying to resit the exams was a no-go. Even if I was to study at evening classes, I just wasn't in the right frame of mind to be successful in academia. I wasn't interested.

The only thing I was interested in was music and acting. I was always listening to music, watching soaps on television such as Brookside, Coronation Street, Crossroads, Emmerdale and EastEnders. I loved them all along with all the varying accents which I would attempt at mimicking whilst watching, which was entertaining for my parents.

However the reality of being pregnant soon hit home. When we received confirmation from our doctor that I was three months pregnant, it was the first time I'd seen my father so visibly upset at this news. I felt as though I'd let everyone down. I felt like I was a huge disappointment and was bringing shame onto the family. However, I wasn't the first girl to get pregnant at such a young age and I certainly wasn't going to be the last.

Decisions needed to be made as to whether I'd keep the baby or put her up for adoption. My parents didn't give me an option. They told me I had a responsibility to look after my child, which I did.

As soon as I had Chanel at the age of 16, I waited nine months before I decided to go out and look for a job. Back in those days, it was maybe a bit easier to seek employment.

Once you showed enthusiasm, determination and that you'd be committed to the job, then you'd be given a chance to prove yourself.

I found my first job in the West End of London working for a company called MacCulloch & Wallis, a fabric and haberdashery shop. I was given the role of switchboard operator/receptionist. I loved it so much. I worked alongside three other ladies in the office and Mr Beresford, who was our office manager. The one thing I remember about Mr Beresford was his very posh accent and his delightful tweed suits.

I didn't tell him I had a child because I thought they wouldn't hire me. So they gave me the job but on a single person's tax code. I worked for the company for around two years. A recession hit and the company tried to find a way to keep me working for them – they asked me to work part-time on the switchboard and part-time in the haberdashery shop. At such a young age, that suggestion felt like a slap in the face, so I declined and took redundancy. Why did Linda not realise the company didn't want her to leave? Linda thought she knew best!

But before that happened, in my first year I received a very large tax rebate and back in those days, we got paid in cash each week. I received at least £350 in cash and it felt as though I'd won the lottery. When I started work, I made a point of paying my parents at least £20 a week from my normal wage each week.

I must admit, I was one of the very blessed young mums out there because I had a multitude of help from my immediate family including a cousin who came from Dominica to live in the UK and she would always offer to babysit Chanel if I ever wanted to go out or if I had errands to run. The gratitude was so real because about a year after I had Chanel, I heard about one of my school friends falling pregnant and her parents asked her to leave the family home and the council ended up housing her and her baby.

So I really did appreciate the continued love and support from my own family in Chanel's upbringing so that I could live as much of a normal teenage life as possible. My parents didn't want me to miss out on my teenage years so they still allowed me to go out with friends while they looked after Chanel.

If my sister and I had invitations to go out to a club and a party over the weekend, we would ask our mum and her response would always be, "Ask your dad and see what he says." When we asked our dad, he would say, "You can't go to both, so choose one and I'll come and pick you guys up at a certain time." Not only did the stress set in for both of us, because we now had to choose between going to one or the other event AND then being picked up in his beat-up Ford Escort! When he parked outside the venue, we would both pretend that our parents had sent us a taxi to collect us. That way, we could hide behind the embarrassment of the car and being collected by our dad!

I look back on the pregnancy and think how lucky, blessed and supported I was. I asked a friend from school to be Chanel's godmother, and she agreed, but it was probably the worst decision I could have made. As soon as we left school, I never heard from her again! One thing I learned was that you don't stay friends with everyone after you leave school and start to make your own way in life.

I still wanted to sing! But how could I when I had a baby? So I started buying the publication called The Stage and looking out for singing competitions nearby in East London.

I wanted to confirm to myself that I still had a little confidence to enter singing competitions. As far as I was concerned, having a baby wouldn't stop me from wanting to become a singer. It might have taken a little longer but I knew that if I had entered these talent competitions, it would give me the added confidence to sing anywhere. My father always drove me to the competitions and sat in the car and waited for me.

At the end of every event, I'd leave the building with a trophy in my hand. I won most competitions and he was never surprised. It was almost as if he expected me to win all the time. I'd get in the car and he would just smile all the way home.

The family and friends events were getting busy. People wanted me to sing at their social gatherings, whether it be a wedding, birthday party, christening or even at a funeral. I didn't mind because it was the only way I could receive positive exposure and show everyone that I was a young teenager trying to continue living the dream of one day working on a West End stage.

The teenage years were rolling over ever so quickly and by the time I was 18 (Chanel was two), I asked my parents to make us homeless so that I could get my own property from the council. Obviously they didn't want to do this, but after much persuasion, before I knew it, a homeless hostel had been found in East London and I took myself and my daughter to our new temporary home. It was horrific.

We had one large main room to live in. It was like a self-contained studio room. The other residents were drug users and alcoholics as well as the odd building contractors who would stay there because of a local job they were working on.

My daughter and I wouldn't stay there during the week because, many times, someone would try and break into our room during the night whilst we were trying to sleep and this was too disturbing for a two-year-old. So we then moved in with my eldest sister, Janet, and we'd go back to the hostel at the weekend to show our faces.

Even the manager seemed slightly off-key and anytime I would talk to him, it was a conversation that was kept to a bare minimum.

Our time at the homeless hostel lasted for around a year before the council housed us in Hackney, East London. This was unexpected because we were now based in a different borough and at the time I thought, 'Oh well, why not'. It was a brand new start for us.

Chanel started school at Mornington Primary and seemed to settle in very quickly – she had the knack of making new friends. I still had to go to work and no one knew of my plight – I was basically homeless, and living in a homeless hostel to obtain a place of our own. On the face of things, I was doing okay for myself and my work colleagues thought I lived the perfect life. How wrong were they were.

3
The 9-5 Single Mum Years

Shelley Berni
Lifelong Friend

So I first met Linda at a charity event my auntie Carole organised in memory of her four-month-old daughter she lost suddenly from cot death.

Linda was a work colleague of my other auntie Marion and Marion had arranged for family friends to come down to the event from London.

Linda sang Greatest Love Of All at the event whilst holding her five-year-old daughter Chanel at the time.

I was in awe of Linda – she sounded amazing.

Marion and Linda continued to work together for a while after if I remember rightly.

I am very close to my auntie Marion so if she was doing something socially I was always invited along. On many occasions this also included Linda and as the years went on we socialised after work, holidayed, had sleepovers and mini breaks together.

Linda has always been so hard-working to provide for her daughter. She used to always be temping in offices and then she would be following her true passion of singing and acting as and when she could as the opportunities arose and came her way.

Whenever Linda secured work with her agent she would always let me know, and where there were the opportunities to be lucky enough to watch her I did at the drop of a hat. She has been on a game show that Aunty Marion went on with her and I was totally honoured when she asked if I would like to go with her whilst she performed on Stars In Their Eyes. The whole experience was amazing.

We have had so much fun over the years and one of the funniest memories of Linda was that we were on holiday and a group were singing Stand By Me in a bar we entered. I don't know why but one of the singers entered the audience and came straight over to Linda. He pointed the microphone to her and she sang the next line to the song. The guy was so impressed but it was so funny as Linda took the mic, finished the song with the other guys and brought the house down! I had everyone coming up to me asking if she was part of the act. I said we had only come in for a drink!

We have had so many fun times.

Linda is a true friend. She is someone who I can just pick up the phone and talk to even if we have not spoken for months.

She always has a listening ear and gives me the best advice, she is so caring and makes me sit back and evaluate situations as I should do.

Linda always makes time for me even when her schedule is crazy-busy.

She is my best friend, great fun, so caring, always happy, hard-working, determined and the best therapy ever.

I love Linda xxx

And the story continues!

By the time Chanel reached 10 years old, I had gone into council tax arrears and was on the verge of being evicted from my home. I had no choice but to return to my parents' home. It was a shame because we loved living in Hackney, however, by the time Chanel reached 10 years old, her mouth was like a sewer. She was picking up street talk from the local kids and she was as rude as hell with it. I didn't want her to follow in her peers' footsteps and be expelled from school so moving back to my parents home was a blessing in disguise.

I always wondered why I couldn't cope with being an adult, especially paying all these monthly bills! Why didn't anyone explain to me what happens in terms of surviving and how to be a responsible adult?

I too was a child and having my own place was a huge responsibility. I wish someone had sat me down and said, "Right Lin, this is what you NEED to do to keep your home. These bills need to be paid so that you don't get evicted!" I laugh about it now, but life continues to be a huge learning curve for me and I welcome all the daily, weekly, monthly and yearly lessons.

Just before we moved back to my parents' home, when I turned 25, I had to have my tonsils out. By then, I was working for the Prudential Insurance company based in East London.

Before I attended my initial hospital appointment, I was always getting so sick with throat infections (tonsillitis). I'd always lose my voice and never knew why it was happening so frequently. Whilst I was with the consultant, he examined my throat and immediately said: "How soon can you come into hospital? Because we need to remove your tonsils as soon as possible."

"I'm a singer," I made a point of mentioning to the consultant, "so please look after me."

He reassured me that all would be well once he'd done the surgery and that I'd be able to sing again afterwards. Consultants don't like alarming patients, so I said I could admit myself in a couple of days once I had organised childcare.

I went into St Bartholomew's Hospital a few days later. At the time I was seeing a guy and no, it's not worth mentioning his name, because at that moment, he didn't give a shit about me going into hospital. My parents were livid at his lack of care towards their daughter and my forthcoming operation.

I informed my employers about my hospital stay and stated I'd be back to work in two weeks. Chanel was being looked after by the local neighbour who looked after her regularly.

The procedure went well and at that time, patients were given crisps to eat instead of ice cream. Rancid! Only because it was meant to heal the throat quicker. Like fuck it did! It made me even worse. So I refused to eat much whilst I was in hospital. I was there for a week and they realised that I was feeling much better and said I could go home.

So I decided to go to my parents' home to rest. Chanel stayed with Sue (a local friend who babysat Chanel often) and she didn't mind. Just before the second week began, Chanel said she wanted to stay with me at Nan and Grandad's. So within a day or so, Chanel was with me back in the family home.

During the second week of being at my mum and dad's, both my parents were at work and it was only myself and Chanel at home. I felt a little unwell because all of a sudden a blood clot formed in my throat and I ended up vomiting it out. Once this happened, I thought I'd be okay, so I carried on with my day.

I took myself off to the chemist to collect a prescription and whilst there the clot formed a second time and I had to leave the shop and vomit it out again. At this point, I was getting slightly concerned.

Should I start getting worried? Why on earth was this happening? Yes, it was scary and all I could think about was, 'I'm at home with a nine-year-old child and my throat keeps bleeding'.

I managed to get back home and by the time I returned, my throat formed yet another clot and the same thing happened for the third time. I saw a road sweeper and I tried to communicate in some very strange way for him to call an ambulance. However, he thought I was some kind of nut job, so he totally ignored me!

Somehow, Chanel managed to call an ambulance. My mum had got home and by then it was around 4.30pm. Mum said that she would stay home with Chanel.

Whilst in the ambulance, the paramedics decided it was the best thing to take me back to St Bartholomew's so that they could examine what was going on.

That evening, one of the nursing staff said: "Back again, what are you doing here?"

I seemed to be fine. No sign of any more vomiting or blood clots, so I was insisting to the nursing staff that I was okay and that I could go home.

They obviously didn't take any notice of me, and said that I was going to stay in hospital for observation and to monitor whether the bleed happened whilst I was on the ward.

Around 2am the next morning, I felt as though there was water in my mouth, so I spat into a tissue and before I knew it, my throat was haemorrhaging.

I screamed for the nurses to assist me and they acted immediately. They called for doctors to come and examine me, to try and find out exactly where the bleeding was coming from.

I remember wearing a nightgown my mum gave me and it was covered from head to toe in blood. It felt like and probably looked like a chainsaw massacre. There was blood everywhere.

The doctors came to my bedside and had an instrument to try and examine my throat. I could only describe it as a metal tablespoon with a very long stem. They tried putting the tablespoon down my throat to establish where the bleeding was coming from - without success because I was falling into unconsciousness.

I couldn't answer the questions they kept asking to try and keep me awake. They had no choice but get me back into the operating theatre as quickly as possible to stop the bleeding.

Whilst all of this was happening, the hospital called my parents and informed them that I would need to be given the last rites because the bleeding was so bad. I had lost a lot of blood and they feared I might not make it through the second operation.

I went back into surgery and the team managed to stop the bleeding. I woke up on the ward the next day with some form of ball sewn in my throat.

The second operation was a success. I stayed in hospital for another two weeks, my parents visited me and brought Chanel with them. My workplace sent flowers and well-wishes. I missed them and the bants.

Can you believe it, once all of this trauma had settled, the so-called 'boyfriend' at the time was nowhere to be seen either! Needless to say, as soon as I could speak again, I told him to fuck off!

The material ball which was sewn in my throat came out of its own accord whilst my family visited one afternoon and all was well. There was no bleeding from there on in. Praise the Lord!

I returned to work around two months after the entire episode happened and everyone was glad to see me back and being my usual upbeat self!

Now you're probably thinking, what about the singing, acting, entertaining? Listen, that was the last thing on my mind whilst all of that was going on. I was just grateful to be alive and so thankful to the team for saving my life but more importantly, Chanel calling the ambulance whilst I was at my mum's. How she knew their address is still a mystery because no one ever told her what the address was, so how did she know it? Let's call it divine intervention! Amen!

Chanel has always maintained that she should've had a big story in the Newham Recorder (our local newspaper) about what she did, but nothing ever happened. Your time is coming baby girl and when it does you'll be going on Dancing On Ice!! (One of her dreams is to not only meet Torvill and Dean but to work with them on the show. Anything is possible!)

I don't think I participated in any form of singing or entertaining for at least six months after the operation, because it was such a harrowing time and I also needed to let my throat heal properly. I still enjoyed singing (lightly) to myself and learning new songs along the way, but I wasn't prepared to be belting out any big numbers until I felt 100 per cent better, mentally and physically.

Being a single mum suited me, actually. It was time for me to start living my life with my daughter. As I think about it, I believe I was relatively happy at the time. I was working in a full-time job I enjoyed, Chanel was happy in school and making lots of friends.

Don't get me wrong, being a single parent wasn't an easy ride. I still had to pay the bills and do all the adult stuff on my own, but I did it. I had the love and support of my parents whenever I needed them. However, the time came one day, I asked my dad for some money to borrow before my payday. I was at their home and he was washing the dishes. I asked him the question, he turned around slowly, looked at me and said,

"No!" He then turned back round and continued washing the dishes.

The favourite child was no longer! The only thing running through my mind was: "Dad, you are supposed to help me out here, I'm the favourite child!"

So I had to just accept his response without argument and leave with my tail between my legs!

I asked my best friend Marion instead and she lent me the money until I got paid again. From that day forward, I never asked my parents for any financial assistance again.

I moved into my home in Stratford and I ended up working two jobs to pay for laminate flooring in my home. At that point, Mum and Dad could see how hard I was working and they offered to pay half of the cost of the flooring.

At that time, I worked full-time Monday to Friday at the Prudential and at the weekends, I worked as a receptionist at a care home in Bethnal Green. My parents could also see that I wasn't spending time at home with my daughter.

Once the laminate flooring was down, I gave up the weekend job.

4
The Agent Years (Theirs and Mine!)

Simon Adkins
Linda's agent (33 Artist Management)

Where to even begin with LJP. I first heard about Linda from our other client, the gorgeous Steph Parry. They were both rehearsing for the original company of Mamma Mia! The Party and Linda had expressed to Steph that she was looking for an agent.

That's where this incredible relationship started. I remember calling her and asking her what she was looking for in an agent, having already secured a great job.

Within two minutes that infectious laughter got me and I knew we were going to get on like a house on fire. We agreed to meet up and so we first met at a London private members' club in Covent Garden. The meeting was wonderful, we hit it off straight out the gate!

When Linda first started auditioning and taping for projects she lacked a certain amount of self-belief and confidence, which is hard to believe looking at her now. But it didn't take her long to get into her stride and she's gone from strength to strength since that day. She wants to work hard and strives to do the best she can with everything I throw at her.

Since working together, Linda has worked on Hollywood movies, major TV soaps, dramas, comedies and commercials for some of the biggest brands out there and even appeared on Britain's Got Talent!

Linda and I have become such great friends throughout our working relationship, I wouldn't change it for the world! She always makes me laugh and is a very thoughtful and generous person!

The credits Linda now has are such a broad diverse list of amazing jobs and I know it's only going to get bigger and better!! The sky is the limit for LJP!

So, where was I, oh yes!

This new two-bedroomed house was a godsend! It was so lovely, a small two-up, two-down kind of house, basic yet it was ours to start making memories and also to make our home even if it was only on a temporary basis.

I was heading into my 30s and Chanel was in the throes of going to secondary school in Aldgate East. Yet again we had to adjust to living back on home land in East Ham and it felt good. I couldn't quite cope with being an adult and paying bills.

The council stated that they were over-saturated with the demand for temporary housing for local residents, and that my case would be referred to the local Housing Association.

After living in our temporary home for around two years, I was offered a more permanent property from the Housing Association and this too was based in East London, not too far from where we were living.

In the meantime, life was continuing on an even keel and I wanted to try and make a go of getting back into singing and entertaining. How on earth was I going to do this if I didn't have an agent to help me?

I was now at a point in my life where I was thinking I'd like to meet someone and see how I get on with joining dating sites. The dates I went on would either make you cry or laugh out loud. I'll return to those shortly!

In 1999, I decided to enter ITV's hit show Stars In Their Eyes. Well, little did I know what I'd let myself in for. It was the first time I had worked on a television show and I found out that this project was deemed as a professional job because we all got paid to be on the show. This would help anyone wanting to get into the entertainment field as a professional artist, so this status was very welcome for all of us who took part.

The process of being involved in television was incredible. I hadn't experienced anything like it before. I was definitely a 'newbie' and I was living my best life. I had the opportunity of inviting some of my closest friends and family to watch the show in the Manchester studios, so I chose one of my best friends, Shelley, my dad and Chanel. Mum was on holiday.

Once the studio had learned that my dad was in the audience watching, they made an absolute fuss of him and went out of their way to organise a tour of Coronation Street for him. He was very pleased to go along with it all, however, he was totally oblivious to what was going on because he'd never watched Coronation Street in his life! He was still very grateful to be there to enjoy the entire experience of being in Manchester where it all happened. He was (and is still) a very proud father to all of his daughters.

So the show was about to be recorded and each artist had to have a rehearsal and was put into wardrobe for fitting and I also had my boots handmade. The pop star I was going to be emulating was the icon herself, Chaka Khan. The song that was chosen for me was Ain't Nobody, which is one of my all-time favourite songs anyway, so to be singing this on national television just about made my life complete.

There were around five artists per show. At the time of recording the show I appeared in, Andrea Corr from The Corrs had a Number 1 hit single called Runaway. They were flavour of the month. So it was inevitable that the young lady singing The Corrs' hit song at that time would win the show. The production team went as far as to organise a signed picture of the band for the lady who won.

The general public never truly know what goes on behind the scenes when it comes to being part of the creative process for a major television show that's watched by millions of viewers throughout the UK.

I received the biggest cheer from the audience, and my friends and family's faces were a picture. Full of pride watching me do my thing on that stage. I loved every minute of it.

I did my best and my best was good enough. All I cared about was my best friends and my dad was in the audience and that's all that mattered to me at that time.

The show was aired a few months later in the new year (2000) and naturally everyone who knew me was thrilled to see me on television.

As a result of doing the show, I was approached by a Liverpudlian agency. Don't ask me what her name was because I can't remember!

I wasn't signed to her for too long because most importantly I didn't have a Spotlight profile set up and I didn't have much professional experience to be signed to an agent.

However, she was determined to sign me to her agency and represent me and try and get me seen for West End projects.

She managed to get me an audition for The Lion King. Naturally I was so excited to be seen for this incredible show. I had to prepare a couple of songs and meet with them. The casting director gave me a recall (second audition) and felt as though I did well. The role I was being seen for was Rafiki (one of the lead roles). I realised at this point that I wasn't as confident as I thought I was.

I didn't get the job on that occasion, but they told me I'd come rather close. They ended up choosing a South African actress to play the role, which was much more authentic.

So that role didn't work out, however the new agent managed to get me a few more auditions. I didn't get the jobs because I feel as though, even though I had a good enough singing voice, I wasn't truly ready to be performing on a stage, so deep down I wasn't too disappointed. I didn't feel confident either and my self-belief needed some work too.

By this time, Chanel and I were living in Stratford, East London, and settled into our permanent home. We loved it. I was working a full-time job now at a drug and alcohol charity and enjoyed my life.

I then decided to apply for another show called My Kind Of Music which was hosted by Michael Barrymore. This was so much fun. I had the TV bug and wanted to experience working on a different show – again to improve my confidence of singing in public and still on a professional platform.

When time came for me to record the show, the Liverpudlian agent and I had parted ways. Through no fault of our own, but there wasn't much she could do for me. My only regret was never meeting face to face to say thank you for trying to help with my singing career.

So again, it was a process of preparation and agreeing on a song to sing for the show. This show was slightly different because it had a game show element to it, so I asked my friend Marion to join me. Marion's general knowledge is first-class and we did very well.

Halfway through the show, they'd let one of the couples sing their chosen song and my song was Unbreak My Heart by Toni Braxton.

It was a fantastic experience meeting Michael Barrymore and I remember especially they wouldn't allow anyone to talk to him until the cameras started rolling. The production team never knew what Michael would say or do.

By the time it was my turn to sing my song, he completely forgot my name and called me "Bev". I had to tell him, "My name isn't Bev, it's Linda." I felt like a star.

Marion and I just missed out on winning £16,000 by one second! Gutted! But we didn't care, we had the best time. The show was broadcast on ITV about a month after Stars In Their Eyes was aired in 2000 and was received very positively.

Friends and family were surprised to see me on television again and it was great keeping the surprise a secret for a while!

I digress a little here because I feel as though you'd like to hear about Linda's dating escapades.

At this point in my life, I started to think about joining a dating site to meet someone new. I was a little bored of being on my own and wanted to make new friends. So one way of me sorting this out was to join dating sites.

My first date was with a guy who worked as a prison officer in London. We met in Covent Garden for a simple drink and a chat and he had a tendency of talking about his fitness levels throughout the date. I just thought he was very proud of his health and fitness regime.

It was a pleasant enough date, but no spark. We left the pub and he said to me, "Let's walk up here." I then found myself on a frog march, up some hilly street at a pace where I thought I was going to pass out because he was walking so fast in front of me.

We have to remember that I'm only 4ft 11ins, I've got very short legs and this guy was about 6ft 3in so his strides were about as wide as Sasquatch going for a leisurely afternoon stroll without breaking into a sweat.

By the time we reached the Tube station, I was not only breathing heavily, but I was sweating profusely as if I'd just ran a marathon. He was just looking at me quite strangely as if it was normal to be walking so fast. Needless to say, I didn't meet up with him again.

I won't bore you with all the weird and wonderful dates I went on, but I'd still like to share one more.

This guy had his own business and seemed like a nice enough guy, I suppose they all do initially don't they?

He asked me to go out with him for a Sunday roast.

Anyone who knows me will know, Linda loves her food, so I accepted the offer in an instant. We arrived at the pub, and I had to wipe my feet on the way out of this establishment. I ordered salmon steak roast dinner and he had the roast beef. Both looked delicious when they arrived.

Well, I've never ever seen anyone eat their meal so quickly in my entire life! He literally resembled a Henry Hoover whilst eating. His meal disappeared within 10 mins. He ate it so quickly. I think by the time he finished his food, I was still on my second roast potato! Yep, he was that fast.

Needless to say, I ended that partnership the next day!

5
What's It Like Being Married to an Actor?

As you can see, I've done nothing but bang on about what's going on in my personal life! Well, at least it shows you that I'm far from boring and I try to spice up my life in small ways!

I managed to get agents to represent me during my career. I went from an agent based in Liverpool, to one based in Wales, then to two London agents and then finally going solo with my own agency.

At one stage I was with an agency based in London who were not very supportive. I should've gone with my gut and gone with a smaller agency who also offered me representation when I had the chance but because the ones in London were meant to be reputable and successful, I decided to choose them. I'm not going to name them, they're not worth mentioning!

Anyway, overall, my confidence wasn't great and I felt as though the auditions and castings were very few and far between. I wasn't booking the auditions I was going for. I think I may have secured around three or four jobs during my two-year stay with them.

There was no support and yes, I fully appreciate that agents have lots of connections to make within a very busy industry, while also dealing with at least 200 other clients on their books.

However, when one doesn't feel supported, then one's confidence disappears soon enough. If castings and auditions don't come to anything, then it's so easy for depression and anxiety to set in.

I doubted myself so much and even though I had a reputable agent at the time, it means fuck all when you're not booking the work. The agent has done the hard work in getting you in the door, so it's up to the actor to PROVE to the casting teams why they've been called in.

At one point during my time with this agency, I didn't get seen for an entire year. Whether they were submitting me for projects is anyone's guess but I couldn't be fucked by that stage.

So one day, I was at home (in Twickenham at the time) and thought to myself that I might as well set up my own agency.

I had no idea how to even start setting up a business. I contacted Companies House and they gave me some more insight and suggested I set up the business as a sole trader.

By the time my husband (at the time) came home, I said to him: "Guess what I've done today?

"What?" he responded.

"I've set up my actors' agency!" I replied.

"But you don't know any casting directors, producers or directors and you may know a handful of actors..." was his reaction.

"Yes, I know all of that, but I'll be working on it!"

And so it began. I worked from the kitchen table every morning. I managed to get more than 15 adults on my books (at that point, I needed to have a certain amount of actors on my books so I could submit them for all the suitable projects that came in). If they sounded like the right fit for a project, I'd submit them!

Five years on, I was running a successful actors' agency. I was looking after 80 actors at one point. The struggle was real, because Chanel and I realised how tough this industry really is. The competition is fierce and both actor and agency need to be bloody good at what they do to build positive relationships with casting directors in both theatre and screen arenas.

And as I mentioned just now, I was married! My ex-husband came into my life after many unsuccessful dates via those dating sites!

We met in November 2007. It was a whirlwind romance. He had the week off from work and because the first date went so well, we decided to meet up again the very next day. Two dates in two days! Things were on the up, literally! By the end of the first week of meeting, I practically moved in with him in Greenwich!

We got on like a house on fire and by the December we were engaged to be married. Things went that quickly but we didn't care because we knew we wanted to be together. He made me laugh a lot, he was a great listener and problem solver. I always maintained that he should've been a counsellor or worked in the educational or medical profession.

Naturally my parents thought that we were rushing into things too much, but Mum and Dad loved him (and still do) and they gave us their blessing to get married.

The wedding took place nine months later (no, I wasn't pregnant) in Canary Wharf and we had over 350 guests! It was a big occasion and yes I sang as entertainment at my own wedding! It was a banging evening! Everyone had the time of their lives.

Thirteen years went by and by now, life was very different. It didn't help that he was the only breadwinner in the family and he was adamant about me not going out to get a 'normal job' because this was my profession. He was very supportive and I would always be grateful to him for that. But we needed money to pay bills and to put food on the table.

The marriage became a challenge for many reasons I shan't go into here. However, we decided to seek marriage counselling and mediation which helped. It confirmed to me that I loved my husband but I was no longer in love with him. It was a very painful time for both of us and I remember him saying during a counselling session that he would never get married again and never meet anyone again.

I filed for a divorce and did everything myself, including seeking advice from pro bono solicitors in the local area. They advised me on what to do and when to take action with certain things.

However, one thing I do find a mystery to this day – about a month after I'd moved back to my parents' home in East London, we met up for a coffee because I was seeking his advice on buying a property in Liverpool.

Again, he was always helpful and gave the best advice but towards the end of the conversation he dropped the bombshell. He'd met someone else.

My immediate thought process was, "Fuck me that was quick, considering you said you weren't interested in meeting anyone," but what actually came out of my mouth was, "Oh, that's nice, good for you babe, I hope she makes you happy!"

He seemed quite taken aback that I was so calm, but no one meets someone that quickly after being divorced for less than a month! Think what you will.

Anyway, during our time together, my own agency was beginning to thrive. I was taking on more actors and seeing more showcases and setting up meetings with actors to see if they'd like to join the agency.

In the meantime, the marriage was falling apart. We were beginning to grow apart and live very separate lives. It was very difficult to communicate with him. Communication is key in any relationship.

Then one of my clients, Joanna Reyes, died suddenly in a car accident on her way home from rehearsals.

This was such tragic news. I was on a training course in Richmond and got the call telling me what happened. I broke down and had to leave the building and go home.

I called Chanel and my ex-partner to tell them the news. They both came home about an hour or so afterwards. I couldn't work, I couldn't talk to anyone, I just couldn't function at all. I cried for days on end.

Chanel had to contact casting directors and take calls because I couldn't cope. We lost Joanna at the age of 37 and it affected everyone so deeply.

A few days after this news, I still couldn't seem to function, Chanel stayed home to help me run the agency and emails were coming in thick and fast paying respects to the loss of Joanna.

My ex was watching television and was complaining about how ridiculous the adverts were and that the creators must be on some form of drugs. How I didn't lose my shit, I have no idea.

It was at that moment I knew my marriage was over. Negativity is not in my life for a reason and I certainly won't tolerate it from someone I'm married to.

It was all too much, so I filed for a divorce and then I moved into the spare room. We lived very separate lives and I think I cooked meals for both of us, but that soon stopped.

By now my agency was going from strength to strength. I had 80 actors on the books and Chanel left her full-time job to help me run the agency. I acquired an office in Hampton which was perfect for us and we'd get to the office early in the morning to start a full day of submissions, meetings and just doing general admin.

The office was my safe space. If I could have lived in it, I would've done. For a few hours a day, Chanel and I could laugh and work in our little haven, meeting so many incredible actors who wanted to join us.

The agency's reputation was beginning to grow so positively and before we knew it, casting teams were calling us to ask us if we had certain types of actors on our books, and if so, could we submit their details.

Overall the agency did well, but not well enough to keep going. Many of the actors didn't get the jobs and once I had plucked up the courage to leave my own agent, I decided to add myself to my books.

The agency was called PMA LONDON! I can hear some of you say, "Oh my God, it was you!" Yes, I was Helen, who many of you spoke to about Linda John-Pierre to ask about her availability. Not just a pretty face!

I was in the throes of getting a divorce, which took two years to complete. My ex and I were barely speaking by this point but just being civil to each other.

I wrote to the agent at the time (where I'd not been seen for anything for over a year) and informed them that I wanted to leave the agency.

Well, what then came was probably the worst, most unprofessional, spiteful, hurtful, evil, damaging email I could ever had received from an agent. I actually felt as though I was about to throw up when I read it.

The last few lines of the previous agent's email to me were:

> *"Part of me can't be bothered to even start going into it but another part just wants to set a few things straight... perhaps it will ensure some relief to whoever has the great pleasure of looking after you next.*
>
> *As regards to the training and the agent work. You absolutely should train, as soon as possible. Your knowledge on how this industry works is appalling and your people skills, social etiquette, exceptionally bad. Furthermore, if you are trying to be an agent*

and manage other people's careers, this is a very frightening prospect. The fact is, you literally do not know what you are doing and you should think very carefully on it."

Needless to say, we parted ways. Leaving them behind has been one of my best decisions ive ever made.

I have learnt a lot since then, most of which has been on-the-job training and this is where my confidence has grown. Some of us don't have to go to university to become successful actors. If we choose to go down such roads, then that's equally positive and for those who chose not to, then it's equally satisfying when we get the jobs.

At the time though, depression set in. Not a lot was going on in my life. After leaving an agent who spat such venom in her closing email, it took me at least a year to get over what she had said. I had to go on antidepressants to cope with everyday life.

I was trying to make my own agency work and without much success. But this is where we learn, right? I didn't give up on having my own agency and I made it work for as long as I possibly could. The difference being is that I actually cared about the clients who were on my books, they weren't just another number or additional commission.

Words are so powerful and used in such a negative way, they can have lasting and damaging effects in one's life. Thank goodness at the time, I had my ex-partner to support me (before the divorce) and my new venture of becoming an agent. I may not have been the best agent out there but my reputation soon went before me for being one of the genuinely nice ones. The testimonials from the clients and casting teams spoke volumes. We were doing something right!

The divorce came through in the June of 2019. I had managed to secure a role in Mamma Mia! The Party via my own agency and was about to embark on a new chapter!

I was due to start rehearsals with them that June so it was perfect timing in terms of moving back to my parents' home in East London.

I also had to make the very difficult decision to close the agency due to my own health reasons and being mentally affected by all the stress of everything. Thinking back on it now, I didn't realise how angry I was with life and what was going on. Anything Chanel said, I'd jump down her throat until one day, she very kindly pulled me up on my 'attitude'! So thanks for that gentle reminder, Chan.

All the actors were sad to say goodbye to PMA London, but we all knew that we had done our absolute best in looking after them and their careers.

A lot happens within any marriage. I have realised and learnt that we not only have to keep looking after our partners but we MUST continue to look after ourselves.

I can bang on about self-love and self-care, but these are the two most important things to keep us grounded and focussed on who we are as human beings. If we don't love ourselves, how can we love others?

I would like to think that I'm a fairly easy-going person to get on with. I'd also like to think that I'm mindful too. I put others' needs first and ensure everyone else is okay before looking after myself. I guess I learnt this from my mother, who still continuously looks after all of us in her own way.

I'm so incredibly grateful to my parents. I've watched them work so ridiculously hard, set up a family home and they both retired relatively early to enjoy the rest of their time together at home.

Even though I've painted a fairly pretty picture of my married life, there are actors out there who do not receive the support they deserve from their partners.

We are also faced with family and friends who just 'don't get it'! Still asking us to go out for drinks of an evening, when in fact, we ARE WORKING! Or 'maybe we can meet up at the weekend for Sunday lunch'. No babe, I'm still fucking working!

Better still, for those of you who receive opening night flowers and gifts from family, friends and agents.

My family never sent flowers to a theatre for me because that's not their world and they wouldn't understand that that's the thing we do in the industry.

So thank you to all of the agents and friends who have sent flowers to me on opening nights. I'm always very grateful for them!

Spare a thought for those who don't receive the love and support whilst they're trying to work hard at their passion, their lifeblood, their career.

Sharing news of being booked for a job is amazing because everyone is happy and the support is there. However, the contract will come to an end and then the negative comments will set in. "So, when are you going to find a real job then?" or, "When's the next audition?"

We get those types of questions all the time and not just from family but from friends who are meant to be supporting us as well. I'm very blessed that none of my friends have ever asked me such questions, and even if they were to, we'd laugh it off.

So for me, it's about being mindful about how we support our partners who work so hard in an industry that's forever competitive and desperately unsociable. Just by having a cup of tea ready for when he or she comes from the theatre or a nice glass of wine ready for them is sometimes more than enough. And if you don't drink, then a nice cuddle will do.

I created a business looking after other actors' careers. I may not have been experienced within the business and may not have had many contacts, however one thing is for sure, I learnt a hell of a lot along the way and I did it with the utmost care and due diligence, always considering the feelings of others.

We all learn something new every day and I learnt a lot during those five years I managed the agency.

Joanna Reyes

6
New Beginnings

Amba Doughty
(I've known Amba since her childhood)

Linda John-Pierre, where do I even begin?

Firstly, congratulations on writing this book!

I am beyond proud of you and what you have achieved over the past few years, you really are living your BEST LIFE. You are one of the kindest, happiest and most beautiful women (both inside and out) I have had the privilege of knowing and I see and value you as good as family.

There was no forgetting the day I met Linda, WAY BACK when I started attending her academy (called Shining Stars Performance Academy).

She welcomed me with open arms, and I'll never forget the first time she laughed. It was infectious and will always be my favourite laugh EVER.

When attending Shining Stars, my mum would take me in each week, and we just had a natural friendship from the start with both Linda and her daughter Chanel. It's crazy when that happens, it was like we knew each other all along. A core memory I'll never forget was the first time we heard her sing. And boy did she SING.

She sang Mariah Carey's Hero at the end of the certificate/awards day and the whole room was full and you could hear a pin drop. It was silent as she performed, both mine and my mum's jaws were on the floor. I felt like I was in the room with Mariah herself. After the academy ended Linda stayed in close contact with my mum, she was always texting and their friendship grew stronger and we saw each other more like extended family.

I actually remember on my 10th birthday I wrote a song for Linda and sang it to her in front of all my family and friends. It was a song to basically say thank you, as the performing arts school she ran had made me so much more confident in myself. I was feeling super-proud of where I was at with my singing and breathing techniques. The song was to the instrumental of the first song she sang – Hero by Mariah Carey. "There's a hero… Her name is Linda John-Pierre…"

We had such a lovely relationship for years while we lived in London. We met Linda's family and we even had Linda's daughter come stay with us a few nights, who called my mum and dad her second mum and dad. She stayed with us while Linda was away singing on a cruise ship. We often met and went out for food. I remember a specific Chinese restaurant we all enjoyed.

My mum also went on a night out with Linda and told her she MUST stand up and do the karaoke – which she videoed and was sending me through the night.

A few years went by and my mum and dad made the choice to leave London and start a new life in Ashford, Kent.

But the friendship travelled with us and continued to stay stronger than ever.

The next chapter was Triple Threat. I was a model for Linda's new modelling agency (yep, she has done so much in her lifetime)! that was all-inclusive. The people under the agency were not just models, they also had other hidden talents whether it be singing, dancing or acting.

This made it so unique in comparison to other agencies. Her and my mum got closer again through this and we often travelled from Ashford to London to attend the photoshoots and castings.

Unfortunately Mum later got diagnosed with a terminal illness. We stayed in close contact through Mum's fight and we watched from the sidelines, as Linda continued to amaze us with her ongoing talents being recognised.

Since then my mum sadly passed away in 2017 and didn't manage to see everything that Linda's achieved over the past five years since passing, but I **KNOW** she too would be just as proud as I am of everything Linda has achieved since then. I honestly believe she is up there aligning the stars to help us all in her own special little way.

Linda, I can't even put into words how truly proud I am of you and everything you have achieved. From the TV commercials to GMB, to BGT to the amazing Mama Mia! The Party.

To now…your own BOOK. There really is no stopping you and I love and admire you for your strength, willpower and determination to push until you get everything you dreamed of. Carry on smashing it beautiful, I'll be right here for the ride to watch you do more amazing things!

Back to the story...

So I'm back at my mum's in East London. Just about to start rehearsals for Mamma Mia! The Party at the O2 in London and what exciting times ahead. I'd just got divorced and my ex and I had now gone our separate ways.

Sometimes timing is everything! We can't always see what's coming but be prepared for the unexpected, people! It truly was perfect timing and it was (initially) lovely yet strange being back in the family home.

My mum's a feeder so she loves to cook for everyone. But my eating patterns have changed somewhat so I don't really like eating late at night.

Okay so I've realised that I've not given an insight into the jobs I have done over the years, so towards the end of this self-indulgence, I'll add a mini CV and stories as to how, when, where, who and what it was like working on certain jobs. The truth continues!

So here I am, back at my mum's, working on a contract which I have been given for one whole year and I couldn't be happier knowing that I'd be working solidly for such a long time.

We started rehearsals and then we opened the show. At the time I shared the role with another actress. I was given three shows a week and she was given four because she had more experience in the industry than I did plus she had worked on Mamma Mia in the West End and the international world tour.

I enjoyed having only three shows actually because it allowed me to chill out in the VIP room or the dressing room.

I was the alternate, so it meant that I had to be in the building whenever she did her four shows. If anything happened, then I could go on at a moment's notice. Again, all good with me because I was there and I enjoyed being part of the show.

In the December of 2019, we had to close the show because Covid had struck and it was spreading like wildfire throughout the cast. We reopened once cast members were given the all clear and could return to work. The lady I shared the role with, had to leave unexpectedly because she had major health issues which needed addressing urgently.

This meant that I had to take over and do all seven shows a week leading up to Christmas and the New Year. I was nervous about it, but excited at the same time because I'd never done so many shows in one week.

I was the alternate so I had no choice but to get on with it. I remember being asked if I was going to be okay doing all the shows, of course I was, it was my job to keep calm and carry on. Stacey guided me with extra advice on how to pace myself and not go full-out all the time but most of all to enjoy the experience.

Rehearsals ended up being an eight-week period of growth and development for the entire cast including the band. We worked with both the Swedish director (Roine) and British director (Stacey). Both had fantastic ideas, and both created a show like no other.

Because I was the alternate, the other lady who I was sharing the role with wasn't always forthcoming with wanting to run through scenes and songs etc. Her response would sometimes be, "Oh, let Linda do it first" and then by the time it was her turn to rehearse the scene or songs, we would be going into tea break, lunchtime or home time.

This was a repeated occurrence with her and I didn't mind at all because it meant that by the time the show officially opened, I was more ready than she was.

More often than not, she didn't really follow the script verbatim in rehearsals and during a live show and when we received notes as a collective, however, not much changed.

At one point I was told that I had to do a speed line run-through with a cast member to ensure that I knew all of my lines. Not only was that an insult to what I was already doing, because I was following the script verbatim anyway, but to be told to do a line run-through, this absolutely broke me. I was so upset. Probably the second most upsetting moment I'd ever experienced within a theatrical contract and to do with something I had no control over. Something like that stays with you for a very long time . It made me feel disappointed, let down, betrayed and not supported. I got over it, and carried on with the contract.

Being the only person of colour in the show was something I couldn't escape. No one feels more isolated than this, especially when it is so visible in cast group photos.

To some, this may not be a big deal but being the only person of colour in any production is a big deal. I would be asked by so many guests, mostly Caucasian people, why I was the only person of colour in the show.

Of course, I had to answer this question very diplomatically, but if truth be told, I didn't have a fucking clue. I'm a mere actor they chose to be in the production and I have proven myself to be hard-working; someone who aimed to do a kick-ass job for seven shows a week. I believe I fulfilled my share of the bargain of trying to be consistent in what I was paid to do.

I'm not going to say any more on this matter because it is in the past and I have been blessed to have worked on the show for three years all bar Covid.

The New Year arrived, 2020 was now with us and we returned to do the show after the festivities. However, news was spreading very quickly about this virus called Covid-19, which was now making its way across the globe very quickly.

By the time the virus arrived in the UK, and just before the 18 month lock down. Cast and crew were catching the virus left right and centre. So by the time lockdown happened, for me, it was a relief to take time out and be at home with my parents for a short while .

I remember our last show and we did the show with an audience of 170 people who were scattered all over the taverna, so it felt as though we were doing a show to a very empty house. This was soul-destroying. By the time we were going to reopen again, we were back in a longer lockdown.

By then everything had gone through with my flat in Liverpool and it made sense for me to move there to start the refurbishment process. So when the lockdown happened, it was more than enough reason for me to decide to go to Liverpool and be in my own home to refurbish it and start making it mine.

There was a lot of work to do but I didn't care, I was on my own, it was my home and Liverpool was now where I belonged. I even checked with the solicitor and she said that I should move in, it was mine now so there was no holding back, I left East London and moved in.

It always makes me smile when I'm on the train from London to Liverpool and when it reaches Liverpool Lime Street station, a sense of being home washes over me.

This really did feel like a new beginning for me. The lockdown couldn't have come at a better time. I was shattered, vocally, physically and mentally.

I would like to consider myself 'old school' and one who works hard and gets on with the job, keeping my mouth shut and not wanting to rock any boats. But I have found that as I've got older, my attitude is changing slightly to that of speaking my truth whether it offends or hurts other's feelings.

I've realised that after being a "yes" person for so many years, it was now high time to say, "Fuck off" or more politely, "No thank you" to people and things that don't serve me.

If something or someone does not benefit my life in a positive way then I've no choice but exclude them from my world and that includes family.

Life really is too short to be putting up with human beings who cause so much unnecessary shit and make your life and theirs a misery! So many people have asked me, "But Linda, how come you're still single, you could have your pick of anyone?" But at the end of the day, I'd rather be single than be with a person who makes my world sad.

Since being on my own, I've realised that self-love and self-care are key to everyone's mental state of mind. Loving on yourself, looking after yourself, treating yourself, taking yourself out to dinner, or to do a little retail therapy is the best love we can give to ourselves. I learnt this the hard way. Sometimes we can be at home, listen to the music of our choice, cook some tasty food, wear your favourite clothing and this simple act could easily make anyone's day.

This then promotes inner happiness, inner peace and inner contentment, which in turn results in a higher confidence level, positive self-esteem, and self-belief.

Confidence mixed with gratitude is key! When you have this mix, then ANYTHING is possible.

7
Liverpool Life!

KK Harris
Lifelong friend
(aka sister from another mister)!!

When I met Linda, it had to be in 1999.

We both had been cast in The Blues Brothers Meet The Soul Sisters and I remember how she laughed in a way that I had never heard before. In fact, when she laughed, I couldn't help but laugh out loud myself.

I honestly felt a sisterly connection because of her laugh. I made sure I had my jokes in tow because I wanted to make her howl. I'm not surprised she's called her memoir Still Laughing because through the ups and downs she's been through; Linda continues to find the humour in life.

I think Linda's laughter is her special sauce and everyone wants more once they've had a taste.

I left the entertainment industry and pursued a different path 12 years ago, however, Linda and I remained close. Linda continued pursuing and living her dream and I have watched her go from strength to strength, gracing some pretty impressive stages like the London Palladium recently in The

Secret Garden, a one-off performance produced by Jamie Lambert, where her performance was a stand-out. "That's my friend," I squealed to those sat near me.

Linda deserves all the love she receives from the audiences she performs to because she is there for the people.

Our friendship is magical and my daughter has a wonderful Godmother who is a very good example of the 'modern woman", living life to the fullest and having it all.

I'm excited to see what happens next for Linda because I am sure it will be big!

Loads of love Linda x

KK Harris

So the refurbishment is taking place. As some of you may know, refurbishing a property isn't always as plain sailing as we'd like it to be, but I had a lot to learn doing this project as a one-man band.

The project was more of a challenge to complete because of the Covid situation. So many companies were so busy they didn't have time to visit to give quotes and when they did, the prices were through the roof.

The kitchen was replaced, flooring replaced, brand new furniture, and the bathroom was the last room to be done. I managed to find a bathroom fitter and he ran off with my money (to get the goods)! However, his behaviour was suspicious when he kept on stating how many cameras were in the main reception area! No shit, Sherlock! It's to keep conmen like you out!

Anyway, he didn't even get halfway through the job when he completely and utterly disappeared. The next guy agreed to do the job and he seemed okay initially, but he not only broke the toilet, he expected me to pay for it. There was a disagreement and he never came back.

I couldn't find a bathroom fitter for love nor money. It was so stressful but I didn't let that get me down. I wasn't going to let two scabby fuckers ruin my dreams of having a nice bathroom.

In the end of all ends, I asked the guy who'd tiled my kitchen to give me a quote on completing my bathroom.

I am more than proud to mention his name because he was so kind, generous, genuine, hard-working, and he completed the job in no time. Odair is from Portugal and I found out that he is a master tradesman who can fit bathrooms, kitchens and flooring.

So when I buy my next property, I'll be going to him and if anyone is in the Liverpool area looking for someone to do any fittings, he is your man.

It took six months to get the bathroom completed. It was worth the wait.

When the job was finished, I found myself getting up and getting into a routine – coffee, breakfast and watching television. Watching television was not my thing. I now felt the need to get out and go to work, even during a lockdown.

I went to some of the high street shops to hand in my CV (such as Lush, Poundland, TK Maxx, Iceland) and no one contacted me, not even to say they had no vacancies. So I went online and found a job as a customer services assistant at a Covid test centre.

Soon enough I was based at the site in Crosby, just north of Liverpool. I didn't realise at the time that anyone could request set shift patterns so that you know your exact hours for the week.

Because I was still technically available to do my acting, my agent (Simon) would still submit me for projects and see what would happen. If a casting arose, it would be via a Zoom call.

I was very nervous about starting at the Covid test site because I didn't know anyone at all. It almost felt as though I was starting school all over again. My first day was really good, they all made me feel welcome even though I did have a little bit of an attitude! I think someone tried to take the piss out of my London accent and it didn't go down well.

But before we all knew it, even though we were in such terrible times, we would be laughing every single day. There was always something to smile about. We could also visit other test sites to earn extra money doing additional shifts. This would break up the week.

I chose shifts on an 'as and when' basis, but soon enough we all found out that the shifts were going very quickly because the ladies in the main office were giving all the shifts to their mates on the sites, keeping them working. Cheeky! But yeah, we all get it!

So I then realised after working at the Crosby site that the managers in charge would allow you to go for interviews and so on, to focus on your actual career. So I asked for a regular shift pattern so that there was some form of stability and routine happening for me. It also gave me a purpose for getting out of bed every day and going to work.

My job entailed talking people through their Covid tests, which they had to administer themselves. Sometimes it was rancid when people would literally throw up after putting the swab down their throats! But I had a way of getting them to do it in a much safer way without throwing up everywhere.

Don't get me wrong, you can't be in a workplace without drama! There's always drama and this place had its fair share!

Put it this way, I had to end up moving to another site just to get away from the Crosby site for a while. I went to the new site which was called Monarchs Quay and it was even WORSE! No one spoke to me whilst I was there.

It was probably the worst Covid test site I've ever worked at – no other people of colour worked there and I was completely ostracised by the women (all ages). No one really spoke to me during the working shift, aside from a couple of the young guys. I even had to pull up a lady about her attitude towards me. After that, she tried speaking to me and I couldn't be fucked to give her the time of day.

This site was very cliquey and I must admit a majority of the staff made you feel like an outsider! Nobody welcomed me and no one was genuinely nice. But I didn't let that faze me. It's other people's insecurities that come through their personalities, so I continued to walk in my power for the duration of time I worked there. Even speaking to the management about the conduct of the staff fell on deaf ears, because I was given a cock and bull story about why they appeared so distant toward new members of staff. They said it could be related to a high turnover of staff and they couldn't connect with new people because they'd leave and go to another site.

So I ended up going back to the Crosby site and then doing extra shifts elsewhere to make extra cash.

Overall I enjoyed my time there. I also managed to film two feature films during Covid which will be released in 2022 and 2023.

I must admit I didn't really miss working on the show or in the industry. It was just so nice to go home in the evening, have a meal and go to bed at a decent hour. It's the little things that we appreciate more when we can't have them.

My parents thought I was crazy when I told them I was moving to Liverpool. My mum stated the obvious: "But you don't know anyone there!"

Well, it didn't take me long to get to know people and to feel settled in my own space which I now call my happy place, my home and my safe space. I always feel so happy when I'm in my flat.

People always ask me why I moved to Liverpool and I have to say, the city has woken me up to living in a different part of the UK. It's the community feel, the friendliness, the down-to-earth characters that I've encountered who have made me continue to smile whilst I've been living here.

No matter where you live, you're always going to encounter odd-balls and not everyone is going to like you, however, we simply have to make the most of life and where we live.

Being strong enough to make that choice to move to Liverpool didn't take long! It was a no-brainer. The divorce happened and there was no reason for me to stay in London. London has changed so much and I felt it was time to move on and do what made me happy.

It's a scary thing to do but I wouldn't have changed my decision at all.

8
Back to London, Back to Work!

So in July 2021, I received a call from Amanda asking me if I'd like to return to Mamma Mia! The Party. Naturally, I said I'd love to. However, this time the contract would be for one whole year and I would be playing the role of Debbie full-time.

This was music to my ears and accepted with absolute excitement and gratitude. Knowing I was going back to London to play this role my heart was so full of gratitude and happiness because I loved playing Debbie so much.

Within an industry that's forever changing and so increasingly competitive, we don't always get a chance to choose who we work with.

I've been blessed to work with many people and most of them I've developed a great rapport with. I say these words with care and caution because it's not every day you come across human beings who change your life for the better and make you a better person even in a small way.

It brings me back to the very beginning, thinking about the audition process. It was tough, however, I knew at the time I'd be part of something incredibly special.

The casting team knew I could sing, they also had my CV in front of them so they could see I had comedy bones too.

I'd like to thank Björn Ulvaeus (executive producer) and Roine Söderlundh (director) for taking a chance on me (see what I did there), as well as Stacey Haynes (director) for her patience, guidance, support and vision of what she could see within me to be able to create my version of Debbie the Chef. Something I couldn't see until I FOUND who Debbie really was and I guess that was a bit of LJP! Stacey is very straight-talking, this woman pulls no punches! I guess this is a good thing because you know exactly where you stand with her and she takes no shit either!

Dawn Spence (Dance Captain/Grandma) also for her support, guidance, dance captain notes, diplomacy, strength and batshit crazy sense of humour. We've had some giggles in the dressing room and we've been there for each other as well as others too.

No matter what happens in an actor's life, we still have to put the make-up on, get the costume on, and bring that smile, when any one of us could be going through challenging times and when you've got people like Dawn on your side, then please know you are truly blessed to know and work with such a powerful and genuine woman.

Anyway, back to the story. It was time to leave my gorgeous home and move back to London to go back to work.

I was probably more upset about leaving my flat, because it had become my home throughout lockdown and I was finally happy. I had been so blessed to come home at every opportunity, normally on my days off, to be in my happy and safe space.

Moving back to my mum and dad's home wasn't too much of a shock initially because I'd been there the first time around before.

The main thing was getting used to being in a West Indian home again, which was always busy. If she had a busy day ahead, Mum would get up early and start cooking the family meal around 5am. That gave her one less thing to worry about later on.

The one thing I felt when coming back to London was the sense of loss. I felt as though I'd lost my independence a little bit. However, my parents always gave me free rein in terms of letting me live my life and getting home at whatever time I wanted.

I had to get back into the frame of mind that I was going back to work. I felt so grateful that I'd been given an opportunity to work for an entire year on a project I loved.

However, despite her early morning efforts, I never really enjoyed cooking at my mum's. So whenever I stayed in London on my days off, I'd take myself off to a restaurant for dinner or get a takeaway. So much easier but not always good for the waistline!

We (the cast) were back and it was a quick turnaround in terms of getting the show ready to reopen. I never like to speak on behalf of other people, so I will say this, I was very grateful to be back in the taverna and ready to reopen the show as Debbie FULL-TIME! What an honour.

All of the cast returned and we just got on with it. It felt as though we were opening the show for the first time. Very exciting times. I was buzzing!

That was the fun, upbeat side to getting back to work. A lot of the guests thought that we were all out of work for the entire duration of the lockdown and I made a point of enlightening them by stating that actors don't do nothing if they're not "acting"!

Some of us teach, work at other establishments and run our own businesses to assist us with a regular income.

The downside to being back in the show (and any theatrical production) was having to sacrifice evenings and weekends. Not being able to meet for dinner in the evenings or special events that we have to miss out on.

It's an unsociable profession, yet we continue to be a slave to it because it's our lifeblood and our passion.

Before we knew it, THE SHOW REOPENED and we had the best time. I loved every minute of it and knowing that I was playing the role full-time could not make my heart any happier. Gratitude was real.

We were into the swing of things and the show was back!

The one thing I'd always say to myself before I even entered the building was, 'Make sure you laugh out loud at least three times whilst you're here and continue to walk in your power!'

I loved coming home to my mum and dad's after the evening shows and always giving them the stories about what had happened before, during or after the performance.

Some of the things certain guests would get up to would be outrageous, funny, shocking and sometimes downright unacceptable. Either way, Mum and Dad were always entertained with my stories when I got home!

No matter how tired I was, I didn't let that take over. Yes we all get tired but for me, it's about being grateful for working and meeting some of the most incredible people who came to see the show.

Whilst working on Mamma Mia! The Party, the one question I got asked a lot was, "Have you ever been in The Lion King?" It's the one question which gets me so mad.

I must've been through at least 15 auditions for The Lion King (for both the West End and once for Disneyland Paris). I auditioned for the role of Rafiki. It was a great storytelling role and the show is spectacular.

So unfortunately the answer is no, I've never been lucky enough to be in The Lion King and I probably will never be.

Sorry (not sorry) for stating the obvious, but just because it's predominantly an all-black cast, that doesn't mean that all black actors/singers have been in The Lion King.

Right about now I'm kind of rolling my eyes, but feeling happy that I've also educated the uneducated about stereotyping!

9
So, What Have I Worked On and What Have or Haven't I Learnt?

I've left this section until near the end because I wanted to focus on you getting to know who Linda John-Pierre is. The struggles and the good times.

It actually cringes me out talking about the projects I've done because I don't want to sound self-centred, which can easily happen! So if I start sounding up my own arse, I apologise sincerely in advance. This is merely an information exercise!

I'm only focussing on the projects I've worked on which taught me things about myself, my professionalism, and the industry. The good, the bad and the ugly.

I've decided to mention the projects that taught me a lot about the industry, television, film and theatre.

1984 – Singing competitions in and around East London

This gave me the confidence to sing in front of a live audience, whether it be in a working men's club or a church hall. Either way, I had to just get on with it and show them what I was capable of. Winning pissed off some of the professional artists but that was their problem, not mine. I was happy to gain confidence and learn new songs for the next set of competitions coming up. This was also the year I had Chanel, so there wasn't really much I could do or progress from there… but I never gave up.

1995 – My very first unpaid semi-professional production I ever got involved in was The Best Little Whorehouse in Texas

This took place in 1995 and I played the character called Jewel. I believe some cast members got paid, but I wasn't one of them. I didn't really care. All I cared about was being in this show and having a great role to play and singing some amazing songs by Dolly Parton.

I remember having to travel every Sunday to a rehearsal venue in north-west London. It felt like an age to get there and there seemed to be so many people involved in this production.

The organisers were a couple called Steven and Katherine. They were so hard-working and dedicated to putting this show on. The show was put on at the Mermaid Theatre and from what I can remember, we did three shows.

It was the most amount of fun and it gave me an insight into how a show was put together and what I had to learn and how to work as part of a team to create a great production.

My parents came to see the show and thoroughly enjoyed it. It felt like a blur because it was over so quickly. All of us enjoyed the experience and some people stayed in touch with Katherine and Steven to do their next production.

I chose not to get involved in the next show only because of the distance in getting to rehearsals every week. It was a huge commitment and I was a single mum trying to juggle surviving and working a 9 to 5 job.

March 1999 – Stars In Their Eyes (ITV)

I appeared in the hit television series as celebrity singer and international star Chaka Khan. I sang Ain't Nobody and I thoroughly enjoyed myself.

When they were deciding on which song for me to sing, the musical director asked me if I could read music. I told him I couldn't and he said I'd missed out on working with him when they have to record the backing tracks for everyone's songs. I regret to this day not being able to read music because I could've had a very good career (to a certain degree) in singing contestants' backing tracks for the shows.

There's no point in me repeating myself here, however, what I will say is that working in television is the way forward for LJP. I love entertainment full stop, however, there's something to be said about a television or film set that gives me life!

March 2000 – Michael Barrymore's My Kind Of Music (ITV)

This was such a fun experience. Michael was such a lovely man and probably one of the best television experiences I enjoyed.

It was a music quiz show I attended with my long-time friend Marion Lightfoot. I chose Marion to be the person to answer the questions because her general knowledge is superb! Again, myself and Maz had the best day because it was so much fun and seeing how Michael works and what the director wanted to capture as soon as we met him. For those of you who do not know who Michael Barrymore is, he's a fantastic, television host, comic and actor.

July 2000 – Blues Brothers Meet The Soul Sisters

This was the first time I met Keith Strachan – director, and the composer for the Slumdog Millionaire film as well as ITV's Who Wants to Be a Millionaire?

It all began when a friend of mine (Natalie Nyngutin) attended an audition at Keith's home in Essex. He told her that she wasn't suitable for the role and at this point, he was desperate to find the right person for the show. Natalie recommended me, so Keith got in touch and asked if I wanted to audition for the role of ensemble member, but singing all the songs by the legendary Aretha Franklin.

I visited Keith at his home and also met Jenny, his lovely wife. We went through the songs Natural Woman and Respect, and maybe Think. As soon as I had finished singing, Keith asked me how soon I could start rehearsals! I thought he was joking but he was deadly serious. So obviously I laughed out loud. Very loudly!

This was the first time I had worked on a professional theatrical project. It was a six-month tour and I didn't know if I could cope with being away from home, however, soon enough I loved it.

This is the project I learnt so much in relation to knowing the basics of theatrical terminology.

I remember Keith shouting at me a lot because I couldn't remember half the things he was telling me and trying to understand all of this new theatrical terminology made me feel like my brain was fried. I felt so intimidated by those around me who learnt new songs and harmonies so quickly. I was like a deer in headlights. I was so scared about doing this show - limiting beliefs set in, doubt, fear and then wondering whether I should speak to Keith and tell him that I could no longer participate in the show.

Of course, I didn't do that because he told me how long it took him to find someone with a certain sound.

Even though I had done The Best Little Whorehouse in Texas, that show was a blur and I remembered nothing! I really and truly knew nothing, so this was an amazing reboot to my career and I learnt so much from Mr Strachan, the best in the business.

Keith had found a wonderful group of people to work together and once we had all got through the rehearsal period, we were ready to go on the road.

It was a very exciting time for me being away from home and going on a new adventure; travelling the UK, touring in an incredible show and singing some of the most iconic songs sung originally by Aretha Franklin. It was a dream come true.

There's one thing to be said here, I didn't know much at all about the industry. I didn't know who people were, I didn't listen to people's advice (the likes of Keith Strachan). I didn't even know how big a deal it was to work at the National Theatre. A situation arose where I was going through the stages of The X Factor and auditioning for a musical called Caroline, or Change. I got offered Caroline, or Change (at the National) and asked Keith for his advice. I didn't take it and went down the road of The X Factor, which ended pretty abruptly when I just missed out on going to the judges' houses. No X Factor, No National Theatre. Back to square one!

If I had known what I know now, I believe life would have been quite different.

May 2001 – September 2001 – All You Need Is Love (The Queens Theatre, London's West End)

This was my very West End debut. It was a production based on the Beatles' music, and Keith Strachan was director and musical supervisor. It was more of a concert-style show, rather than a West End musical with text. It literally was song after song. I was very fortunate to be given four songs to sing and loved every minute of it.

I still struggled with remembering movement and there was a bed scene with ALL of the cast. I just couldn't even remember my own choreography that we were free to devise, so the team decided to keep me out of that one scene. I felt so stupid and this is where I had wished I'd gone to drama school to learn things quickly.

From then on, I made a point of going to dance classes for beginners at Dance Works and Pineapple Dance Studios.

Attending those beginners classes felt so intimidating because everyone still looked as though they knew what they were doing but more importantly, they picked up the most basic steps very quickly.

All I could think was, 'These people are meant to be beginners, but they know exactly what they're doing'. So because I felt so intimated, I stopped attending the dance classes.

I also went to basic ballet classes but I hurt my Achilles' heel, so I couldn't attend those classes either until I was fully recovered. Once I was better, I didn't bother going back. It sounds as though I gave up rather quickly but, at the time, I believed I couldn't achieve much. Self-belief was not a strong point at this time in my life.

That was a real struggle. Choreography and me are clearly not besties but one thing's for sure now, I will give everything and anything a go in relation to movement, even if I'm wrong and strong!

Over the years I've got (a little) better, and more confident with movement.

February 2007 – Eight-week one-nighter tour – Sweet Soul Music – UK – Director Keith Strachan – Stax and Atlantic Music show

Again, another project led by Mr Strachan, and this time, I was a little bit better with theatre terminology. I was gradually settling into the theatrical world and I started this job after leaving a corporate day job which ended up with me going off sick with depression before Christmas in 2006.

Then I handed in my notice during my time off sick. Never has a day job made me so ill. Never again will I do what makes other people happy. As soon as my notice period was up, I booked Sweet Soul Music in the February and as soon as that tour was over, I booked The Billie Holiday Story.

Sweet Soul Music was a gruelling tour. One-nighters, so this meant that we had to travel to each venue, perform for one-night only and then move onto the next. It was hard work, but I loved it. Time to shine and sing my all-time favourite songs.

Being on the tour also taught me about being patient with others. I realised that I like and enjoy my own company and how confident I am in my own skin to NOT need to be in anyone else's company.

April 2007 – The Billie Holiday Story – UK and Ireland tour

Whenever I start a new project, fear, anxiety and unnecessary stress enters my life. I have OCD anyway, so my thought process is always about getting it right and as long as the director is happy, Linda's happy. My role within this project was playing Sadie Fagan, Billie Holiday's mother in Act 1, and Ella Fitzgerald in Act 2.

The show must go on and it always did, no matter who went off sick. This show was directed by Stephen Leatherland and it was very special because we had Rain Pryor (the legendary comic Richard Pryor's daughter) playing the role of Billie Holiday herself.

The show was beautiful yet challenging in some ways. Some weeks we just about got paid, while once we almost didn't get checked into a hotel because the reception staff said there was no bookings for our group. Thanks to Andrew Venning, who was part of the cast – he spoke to reception and gave every name possible to prove we had a booking there.

I was in my comfort zone now and feeling relatively at ease with what I had to do in this show. I was glad when the tour came to a close because I missed being at home. What did I learn from this experience? Well, mainly to be ready for the unexpected. Rain dropped out of the show very suddenly, so another actress (Ade) had to take over in the role. She did a great job and practically learnt the lines within 24 hours.

2008 – Beautiful People (BBC2)

This was my very first television role. I completely and utterly fell in love with television. The way everyone treated each other. The respect, the genuine kindness and the immense joy from everyone on set. Am I living in fantasy land here? Who knows, but one thing is for sure, I loved this genre of work.

I played a character called Keisha Camille. It was a very small role, however, I loved it. It was my first time working on a television project and it was huge amounts of fun. Lots of waiting around and just being starstruck by watching Olivia Colman and Meera Syal in the leading roles whilst we all did a burial scene by the graveside. The directors (Jon Plowman and Gareth Carrivick) heard I was also a singer and so I ended singing Respect by Aretha Franklin at the graveside.

I learnt on this job that you need to know your shit (learn your lines and the quicker the scene is recorded, the quicker the director can move onto the next scene and get everything done as quickly as possible. It can be quite repetitive with filming the same scene but from different angles.

My taste for screen work grew. I was beginning to feel more at home on a film or television set. Go in, get the job done and go home! Love it!

2009 – 2012 – Chicago Musical USA Production – Allure of the Seas, Royal Caribbean Cruise Line – Mama Morton

The first contract was heaps of fun. Initially it didn't feel like that because I had only been married for six months when I got booked for this job. It was the first time I'd left a country to work and live abroad. I was completely out of my comfort zone and I could not stop crying all the way to the airport. Even whilst at the airport, I was sobbing uncontrollably. The staff thought something terrible had happened.

Never have I felt so alone yet so excited for what was to come. Working on the biggest cruise ship in the world (at the time) and living an independent life. Looking after myself and not relying on anyone to help me work things out.

By the time we boarded the ship, we had already had about four weeks of rehearsals in Fort Lauderdale. We were all living in gorgeous apartments and getting to know each other. Each apartment could house at least a family of six comfortably. I was very lucky, I shared an apartment with three others and we had our own rooms, thank goodness.

I called my husband every evening and informed him how everything was going. Needless to say, my first phone bill whilst away was over £1,200 for the month!

Rehearsals were excruciatingly intimidating. They hired the best of the best from around the world to work on this production. The director was Scott Farris, the musical director was Vinny (Vincent) Fanuele and the choreographer was Gary Chryst.

I struggled so much with learning the lines because I was in awe of working with such an incredible team. To the point where Scott called me in a room one afternoon and said: "You know what Linda, you need to get over yourself, focus on your lines and focus on what you need to do for the show."

Get over what, I hear you ask… Well, me being starstruck by working with this amazing Broadway team. I got over it eventually because the cast made it clear that I was the weakest link in the production and the fact that I was a British actress in an American show on the ship.

Well we actually had two other British actresses who were in the show playing Velma Kelly (Genevieve Nicole) and Roxie Hart (Helen Turner).

What a team! How blessed was I. My gratitude didn't really kick in until we opened the show on the ship and we only did three shows a week – that's when I realised how much free time I would have.

Playing Mama Morton in a 90-minute version of the show was giving me life.

It was whilst I was on the ship that I realised that I didn't like being married. It was an awakening I couldn't dismiss.

More so, when my husband came to visit, he showed me a tattoo he'd had done of my name on his chest. I wasn't happy about it at all. Never would I put someone's name on any part of my body (apart from Chanel which is on my ankle)!

How does one process such emotion and feelings? I lived in my own little bubble on the ship. I lived my best life and my gratitude was real. I was so truly happy with who I was and how I developed personally as a human being who had no choice but to look after herself and her wellbeing.

I was so happy that some of the staff on the ship kept on asking me what I was on. I was high on life because I recognised what I could achieve.

The second contract didn't work out so well. It was a different cast who were in place and so much younger than the original cast.

I hated it. I made an official complaint about one of the cast members – an Australian actor who would talk freely in a racist manner. Sorry, but that's not acceptable ANYWHERE in life or in showbiz.

Because I spoke out about this to the management, the entire cast ostracised me for the whole contract. It was hell. The only person who didn't really want to take sides was a lovely lady who had the role of Velma Kelly and her name was Zara. Zara came from the UK too, so it was comforting to have her on my side at times.

I felt alone, angry, frustrated and fucked off at other people's behaviour towards me. But I didn't let it get me down. It didn't stop me from enjoying my contract. I hung out with other staff members from different departments and worked extra shifts on my days off so that I kept busy.

Working so many hours and making friends in other departments got me through the contract. I surrounded myself with like-minded people who were living in gratitude and happy with their life and work on the ship.

2013 – A Mad World, My Masters – RSC – Stratford-upon-Avon – UK Tour and Barbican – Director Sean Foley

I had a blast working for such a reputable company. The Royal Shakespeare Company is a dream – if you manage to work for them, you've made it! The production and cast were phenomenal. I felt very grateful to be part of something special.

I auditioned and very similar to the Keith Strachan situation where he was struggling to find a good singer, I came along and sang Natural Woman at the audition in front of the musical supervisor Ben Ringham and some of the production team.

The same day, I was informed that they would like to offer me the role of jazz singer in their production of A Mad World, My Masters – a Jacobean farce and stupidly funny! We all had heaps of fun on this project.

However, halfway through our contract, I realised that my details were right at the back of the programme (playbill to some). I made a complaint about this and the company had new programmes printed.

My argument was I was an actor, playing a jazz singer in a show.

The show toured the UK and I enjoyed it a lot. What a blessed time to work for such an establishment. That memory will stay with me forever.

2015 – Showboat – Crucible Theatre (Sheffield) then New London Theatre (now the Gillian Lynne Theatre), West End. Director Daniel Evans

This show was so magical. The set, the costumes, the music, the cast were truly outstanding.

My role was first cover Queenie/Ethel and Old Lady. However, I developed the worst anxiety in working on a theatrical production. I felt physically sick.

It started when we had to go through understudy rehearsals and at this point, I had to do the role of Ethel. Hated it! I fucked up so many times, it wasn't even funny. You know in an instant that people judge you no matter how much they like you.

I had found the job myself, so at the time, I thought, 'Oh this sounds like heaps of fun'.

But then the time came for me to go on as Ethel and I got completely flustered and got most things wrong. Standing in the wrong place most often! On one particular day, once the show had finished, the resident director (not worth mentioning her name) came into the dressing room where all seven of us ladies were sitting and proceeded to shout at me in front of everyone. It was completely humiliating.

Admittedly, I said something on stage (I can't remember what) which was funny to the cast but not funny to the creative team. I apologised to the director and resident director, however, this has tarnished my reputation somewhat and I've never worked with him again.

The resident director could've asked me to leave the room to have a private conversation about my actions. This didn't happen. That incident shook me to the core and I chose not to work in theatre for the next three years.

I almost jumped for joy when we were informed that the show was closing three months later in August of 2016.

2019 – EastEnders – Director Waris Islam

This was so much fun. Scary to work on set with such a talented bunch of human beings who have worked on this iconic BBC TV show for so many years. EastEnders has been a favourite television soap of mine since it began. I had a small scene playing Rose Bartley, who was a talent scout for beauty pageants.

This was a very quick turnaround and luckily for me, we got the scene recorded in about two hours. This gave me enough time to get back to London and do an evening show of Mamma Mia! The Party. It was a long day because I had to make my way to the BBC studios by 6am and I left by midday.

I was elated, buzzing off life and knowing that the scene I recorded would be on television in a month or so. It was transmitted on 9th December 2019.

It is my dream to be a regular in a soap, I don't mind which one because I know my career would reach new heights if this happens. The self-belief is there now and no one can take that away from me.

I have made a point here to mention projects I've worked on that have filled me with complete joy and gratitude and I've also written about jobs that made me sad. It's clearly evident that the industry isn't always a joy to be part of. However, I'm grateful for all the lessons learned including running an agency and being dropped by agencies.

We are human too and go through so much shit. The general public would never know what goes on behind closed doors and some of us have been through such life-changing, happy, harrowing, tragic, stressful times, yet we carry on for the sake of the show.

The following projects were the most fun and enjoyable to work on. I can't mention every single one because the book would be very long, but these projects meant the world to me to have worked on them and worked with such extraordinary, awe-inspiring, astonishing people.

2018 – Angel Has Fallen – Feature Film – Director Ric Roman Waugh (Role: Receptionist)

2019 – Aladdin – New Wimbledon Theatre – Director Kerry Michael (Role: The Empress)

2021 – Cinderella – Feature Film – Director Kay Cannon (Role: Anastasia)

2021 – Alma's Not Normal (BAFTA WINNER) – BBC2 Comedy – Director Andrew Chaplin (Role: Siobhan)

2021 – Mecca Bingo Television Commercial – Director Chris Mudge (Role: Mabel)

2022 – Disenchanted – Disney Movie – Director Adam Shankman (Role: Nosey Neighbour)

2023 – Greatest Days – Feature Film – Director Coky Giedroyc (Role: Linda Jackson, Nurse)

2022 – People's Postcode Lottery – Television Commercial – Director Joe Roberts)

2022 – confused.com – Television Commercial – Director Jake Dypka

2022 – The Secret Garden at The London Palladium Theatre (one-off performance) –

Director Nick Winston

2022 – (This had to be the most fun I've EVER had in filming for a major daytime television show) DOCTORS – BBC1 – Director Niall Fraser (Role: Mona Beckford)

10
What Does Chanel Have to Say About All of This?

Here we are, my mum has asked me to write something about who she is, our relationship and what it's like being Linda John-Pierre's daughter.

From an early age, I've always loved performing arts. However, my love is for dance –particularly contemporary and urban street dance.

Even though Mum attempted to take me to ballet classes, I hated it, so she didn't push me any further and allowed me to just stay home and play with my friends and dolls.

Well what can I say... Mum I'm beyond proud of you for writing this autobiography...

I'm going to take it way back to when you had me when you were 16 years old. Throughout my childhood I remember having it all.

I was very well looked after; you worked your ass off to ensure I never went without. Please believe I will be forever grateful to how I was raised. Even though times were hard, you just got on with it which again showed me what a strong woman you are.

I would look up at you and think, 'Wow I'm so lucky you are my mum'. I still think that now actually!

I will never forget when I was nine years old and you had your tonsils out. You were sent home and lo and behold you started to haemorrhage in your throat, and I had to tell the 999 emergency response team where we lived, and at the time we were staying with Nanny and Grandad.

I had no idea what their home address was but it just came to me. Thinking back on it now, it was absolutely awful for a nine-year-old child to witness and deal with such a traumatic event, let alone it being my mum.

The ambulance team arrived and all I could think of was, 'Please save my mummy, please'.

I SAVED your life, how on earth I didn't end up in the local newspaper (The Newham Recorder) or on ITV News, I will never know. ***I SAVED YOUR LIFE MUM!*** Before long, you were home (for a second time) and you made a full recovery.

When I was around 14 or 15 years old, I got my tongue pierced. I made the appointment on the same day, rushed home, rushed through the door as though something urgent had happened and said: "Oh my God Mum, I need £40, I've just booked to get my tongue pierced!"

You looked at me in absolute horror but you still gave me the money to get it done. My friends were like: "Chan, your mum is well cool, how has she just given you the money just like that to get your tongue pierced? I want your mum to be my mum."

Another memory I have is when we went to New York. This was when you got your very first tattoo done on your ankle and in colour, I mention this because British tattooists like tattooing people of colour's skin… It's been a struggle.

I was so excited for you and that inspired me to want one when we got back to London. So as soon as I turned 15, boom! And just like that, you gave me a voucher to get my first tattoo. I was overjoyed and super grateful. Again, my friends said: "Chan, your mum is so so cool, my mum would never let me do that!" As a tribute to my mum, I got music notes all the way down my back. Yeah it killed, but it was well worth it!

Whilst growing up, you taught me about having manners, respect and love for others, however, I also knew never to take any bullshit and how to stand my ground. Hence why sometimes people would say I have no filter and say things how it is… I guess that's the East End in me coming out! What you see is what you get with me.

Mum, you are my hero, my best friend, my everything, forever making me Laugh Out Loud, we have the best laughs and that's because you think you are man dem... (A true road girl) (In-joke – Mum thinks she's down with the kids!)

I know I haven't always been the easiest of human beings to get on with, however, my love for you will never die. You taught me so much and for that I will always be truly grateful and humbled.

I remember when you cuddled me (still do) and pretended you were stuck, it was the cutest thing and also made me chuckle.

However, ultimately, you are such an inspiration to me and so many. I find it overwhelming that anyone we meet automatically wants you to be their mum – to me it's an adorable thing.

I'll always remember the events, shows, auditions and most importantly working with you when we had the actors' agency (PMA London).

Those days I will cherish forever – what an experience that was. We didn't have a fucking clue what we were doing, but we learnt along the way, even with me leaving my day job to work with you for no money so that the agency could become a success, and it did!

The people we met along the way will forever be amazing memories... The shows, how could I forget the showcases and the graduates seeking representation.

Trying to convince them to join our agency, they'd decline us and then a few months later, they heard on the grapevine that we were getting our clients seen for projects like Game Of Thrones, projects for ITV, BBC, Channel 4 etc as well as Netflix. So they'd reconnect with us asking if we would reconsider representing them. What do you think we said?

Forever grateful to have experienced this all with you, because when I think about those times, I continuously feel truly blessed and inspired. We couldn't even pay ourselves, but we had the best time doing what we did, in the little office in Hampton, building a reputable agency.

Let's talk about some of the shows you have been in, where do I even start? I'm not sure if we've got time to offload so much information about how grateful I am to have seen you in all the shows you have performed in.

It literally blows my mind, just thinking about it! Truly spectacular.

But what I would say are my favourites which spring to mind are Blues Brothers Meet The Soul Sisters and Showboat. I was totally blown away. So moving, emotional and just brilliant. The cast were fantastic too.

When you told the family that you'd got the role of Mama Morton in Chicago the Musical, on the Allure of the Seas Royal Caribbean Cruise Lines, that was a moment I thought, 'This is it. My mum's made it!'

Well, I simply had to visit you to see what all the fuss was about! And what an experience that was for you (and for me). Not having you around for such a long time was a challenge but when we got invited to visit you on the ship I made a point of living my best life.

EVERYONE, from the Captain, through to the bar and restaurant staff absolutely loved my mum, including the housekeepers who cleaned the cabins. They all made a point of watching my mum in the show and of course, they loved her!

It's not just about watching my mum do what she loves, it's the fact that people just LOVE my mum and I can see why. If she's not making you laugh, she'll be listening to your problems without judgement and helping you find the solutions. It was such a magical experience. I will never forget it.

I'm beyond proud of you and forever will be. I'm also very grateful to be on this amazing, incredible journey with you. Sometimes I feel as though I can't keep up with all the projects you continue to book and I catch myself saying, "WOW, MUM, THIS IS IT" and, "Here you go again, killing it, doing what you love."

Mum, all I've ever known is you being a grafter, you continue to work so hard, your work ethic is mental... Always getting those self tapes in and before the deadlines because you and I know the competition out there is fierce, now more so than ever.

Mum, keep doing what you love, you are an inspiration to us all, including myself.

Nanny and Grandad as well as other family members are just in awe of you and your work ethic.

By the way, I can't see my mum hanging up her performing boots just yet.

Just keep doing what you're doing. I love you, we all love you so so much...

Love Chan xx

Fine dining with the wealthy. Gold-plated forks and knives. This is where I started in the restaurant industry in 1993 as a part-timer. The restaurant had a live band and classic ballroom dancing—the experience was like theater to me. Raised in a middle-class family, I loved and was astonished by the glamour, showmanship, restaurant design, and elegant food presentation. My job was to polish cutlery and stack clean dishes when they came out of the dishwasher. Still, I asked the management to train me in the kitchen, dining-room service, and management. I wanted to learn everything about the restaurant business.

Inspired by that experience, I knew I had found my calling and decided to pursue the food and beverage industry after high school. I studied the American Hotel and Hotel Association Educational Institute courses in food and beverage management. In my studies, I learned about fine dining and classic cuisine from chefs Marie-Antoine Carême, Auguste Escoffier, and Paul Bocuse. My dream was to become the food and beverage director of a luxury five-star hotel.

She is clothed
with Strength
and
dignity and
laughs
without
fear of the
future.

Proverbs 31:25

Photos

1973 – Mum (Outside house in Pragel Street, East London

1975 – Family portrait- in East London

1986 – Mum and Chanel (aged 2 years old)

1986 – Linda and Chanel

1992 – Linda and Chanel (Hackney Years)

2000 – Linda's Headshot was taken by Jennie Scott Headshot Photographer

2000 – Linda and Matthew Kelly – Stars in Their Eyes, ITV

2000 – Linda Karime Kendra and Dawn Hope (Blues Brothers Meet The Soul Sisters)

2000 – All You Need is Love West End Musical

2009 – Mum, Dad and I on cruise ship, Allure of the Seas (Royal Caribbean Cruise Lines)

2017 – Linda and Shelley Berni – Linda's 50th Birthday celebrations

2019 --Linda and Chanel

2019 – Linda and Matt Lucas (at Mamma Mia the Party, O2)

2019 – Linda's debut appearance in Eastenders as Rose Bartley

2019 – Linda (Debbie the Chef) in Mamma Mia the Party

2021 – Linda in Well Behaved Women. Photographer: Michael Wharley

2020 – Linda in Mamma Mia the Party – Picture taken by Richie Zamorksi

2020 – My Happy Place – In Liverpool

2022 – Linda and Lucy Benjamin – in BBC1 Doctors

2022 – Linda and Alison Hammond – This Morning with Mamma Mia the Party

2022 – Linda with Ant and Dec in Britain's Got Talent

2022 – Linda on Britain's Got Talent

Made in the USA
Las Vegas, NV
11 January 2023